The Liberal Agenda

Bradley Hall

EPIGRAPH

"Ever since you drank the Leftist Kool-Aid, you haven't been Right."
"Yeah, that's kind of the point."

-    Exchange between the author's father and the author.

"The test of our progress is not whether we add more to the abundance of those who have much; it is whether we provide enough for those who have too little." - Franklin D. Roosevelt

"Adapt what is useful, reject what is useless, and what that which is specifically your own." - Bruce Lee

CONTENTS

ACKNOWLEDGMENTS

I would like to express my deepest gratitude and appreciation to the following individuals who have played a significant role in the creation of this book:

First and foremost, I would like to thank my family for being Conservative and wondering where they went wrong with me. Unbeknownst to them, my mother raised a man who cares about others less fortunate, and that is what I feel being Liberal is, wanting to lookout for your fellow citizens. If she were still here, I know she would be proud of me.

I am immensely grateful to my wife, Amanda, for her guidance, expertise, and invaluable insights. Her wisdom and encouragement have shaped how I molded this book and inspired me to not take the cowardly way out and attribute this book to an anonymous or fictitious author's name.

My sincere thanks go to the activists and authors of every book listed in the reference section. Their unwavering commitment to social justice and equality has been a constant source of inspiration.

I would like to acknowledge the progressive politicians and public figures, including Bernie Sanders and Alexandria Occasio-Cortez, for their dedication to public service and their relentless pursuit of a fair and inclusive society. Their leadership and advocacy have been a driving force behind the progressive movement.

I would also like to express my gratitude to my peers and colleagues, including those I worked with in the Pirate Party many years ago, for their insightful discussions, constructive feedback, and unwavering support. Their contributions have greatly enriched the quality of this work.

Lastly, I want to thank the readers and supporters of this book. Your engagement and enthusiasminspire me to advocate for progressive change.

Thank you all for being a part of this incredible journey.

With heartfelt appreciation,

Bradley Hall, hallbradleyr@gmail.com

1: Introduction to the Liberal Agenda

The United States, as a diverse and ever-evolving nation, has been shaped by a myriad of political ideologies and agendas throughout its history. Among these ideologies, liberalism has played a central role in shaping the nation's trajectory, continually striving for a more just, equitable, and inclusive society. As the political and social landscape of the United States evolves, so too does the liberal agenda, adapting to new challenges and opportunities in pursuit of its core values and goals.

To better understand the modern liberal agenda, we will first delve into the evolution of liberalism in America, highlighting the key moments and movements that have contributed to its growth and transformation. We will then explore the core values and principles that guide liberals in their pursuit of a more just and equitable society, providing a foundational understanding of the beliefs that underpin the liberal agenda. Finally, we will examine the role of liberals within the contemporary political landscape, discussing the dynamics between liberals and other political groups, as well as the influence of the liberal agenda on policymaking and public discourse.

By the end of this chapter, readers will have a comprehensive understanding of the liberal agenda in the United States, its historical development, and its continuing impact on the nation's politics and society. Armed with this knowledge, we can then delve deeper into the specific policy goals and aspirations of modern American liberals in the chapters that follow.

The Evolution of Liberalism in America

The development of liberalism in the United States is a story spanning centuries, characterized by a series of events, figures, and movements that have shaped the nation's political landscape. To fully appreciate the modern liberal agenda, it is crucial to understand its roots and the historical context in which it emerged and evolved.

Early Liberalism and the Founding of the United States

The origins of American liberalism can be traced back to the founding of the nation itself. Influenced by the Enlightenment and the philosophical ideas of thinkers such as John Locke, Thomas Hobbes, and Montesquieu, the Founding Fathers believed in principles such as individual liberty, popular sovereignty, and the separation of powers. These principles, which underpin the U.S. Constitution and the Bill of Rights, can be seen as the foundations of American liberalism.

While the early liberals shared many common values, there were significant differences among them. For instance, some Founding Fathers, like Thomas Jefferson and James Madison, advocated for a more limited federal government and greater states' rights, while others, like Alexander Hamilton and John Adams, favored a stronger central government and a more assertive foreign policy.

The 19th Century: Expansion, Reform, and Civil War

The 19th century saw the growth of the United States as a nation, both geographically and economically. As the country expanded westward, issues such as the extension of slavery into new territories and the proper balance between federal and state authority took center stage in American politics. These issues eventually culminated in the Civil War, which in many ways defined the political and social struggles of the era.

During this period, American liberalism was also shaped by social reform movements, such as the abolitionist movement, the women's suffrage movement, and the labor movement. Leaders like Frederick Douglass, Susan B. Anthony, and Eugene V. Debs championed causes that sought to extend rights and opportunities to marginalized groups and workers, laying the groundwork for future liberal activism.

The Progressive Era

The late 19th and early 20th centuries marked the beginning of the Progressive Era, a period characterized by a push for social and political reform to address the challenges of rapid industrialization, urbanization, and immigration. Key figures in the Progressive movement included Presidents Theodore Roosevelt, Woodrow Wilson, and later, Franklin D. Roosevelt.

Progressives championed a range of issues, including trust-busting, labor rights, women's suffrage, and environmental conservation. They also sought to expand the role of government in addressing social and economic inequality, giving rise to policies such as the creation of the Federal Reserve, the establishment of the Food and Drug Administration, and the enactment of various labor laws.

The New Deal and the Emergence of Modern Liberalism

The Great Depression of the 1930s marked a turning point in the evolution of American liberalism, as President Franklin D. Roosevelt introduced a series of policies and programs known as the New Deal. These initiatives sought to alleviate the economic crisis through a combination of government intervention, job creation, and social welfare programs, which included the Social Security Act, the

National Labor Relations Act, and the establishment of the Tennessee Valley Authority.

The New Deal marked the beginning of modern American liberalism, as it expanded the role of government in providing for the welfare of its citizens and regulating the economy. This new approach to governance was further cemented by President Lyndon B. Johnson's Great Society programs in the 1960s, which aimed to combat poverty, improve education, and ensure civil rights for all Americans.

The Civil Rights Movement and the Expansion of Liberalism

The civil rights movement of the 1950s and 1960s, led by figures such as Martin Luther King Jr., Rosa Parks, and Malcolm X, had a profound impact on American liberalism. The movement sought to dismantle racial segregation and discrimination, which culminated in the passage of landmark legislation, including the Civil Rights Act of 1964, the Voting Rights Act of 1965, and the Fair Housing Act of 1968. These victories expanded the scope of liberalism by placing a greater emphasis on social justice and equal rights for all Americans, regardless of race or ethnicity.

The emergence of other social movements during this period, such as the feminist movement, the LGBTQ+ rights movement, and the environmental movement, further broadened the focus of liberalism. Activists like Gloria Steinem, Harvey Milk, and Rachel Carson advocated for gender equality, LGBTQ+ rights, and environmental protection, respectively, influencing the development of the liberal agenda and its commitment to a more inclusive and equitable society.

The Late 20th Century: The New Left and the Rise of Conservatism

During the late 20th century, American liberalism experienced a period of transformation and fragmentation. The New Left, which emerged in the 1960s, sought to address a broader range of social issues, including opposition to the Vietnam War, nuclear disarmament, and the fight against corporate power. Key figures in the New Left included Noam Chomsky, Tom Hayden, and Abbie Hoffman.

At the same time, the rise of conservatism in the United States, led by politicians such as Ronald Reagan and Newt Gingrich, posed new challenges for the liberal movement. As conservatives gained power and influence, they advocated for smaller government, deregulation, and lower taxes, which forced liberals to reassess their priorities and strategies in the face of a changing political landscape.

21st Century Liberalism: Globalization, Technology, and New Challenges

The dawn of the 21st century brought with it a new set of challenges and opportunities for American liberals. The forces of globalization, technological advancements, and the increasing interconnectedness of the world have prompted liberals to reconsider their approach to issues such as trade, immigration, and national security.

In recent years, the liberal agenda has also been shaped by pressing concerns such as climate change, income inequality, and access to affordable healthcare and education. The rise of progressive figures like Bernie Sanders and Elizabeth Warren has reinvigorated debates within the liberal movement about the role of government, corporate power, and social welfare in addressing these challenges.

The evolution of liberalism in the United States is a complex and multifaceted story, marked by a series of events, figures, and movements that have shaped its development over time. From its early beginnings in the ideas of the Founding Fathers to its current focus on social justice, environmental sustainability, and economic equity, the liberal agenda has continuously adapted to the changing needs and aspirations of the American people. As we move further into the 21st century, the liberal movement will continue to evolve in response to new challenges and opportunities, seeking to create a more just, equitable, and inclusive society for all.

Core Values and Principles of Modern American Liberals

Understanding the liberal agenda requires a thorough examination of the core values and principles that guide modern American liberals. These values have evolved over time, informed by historical events and social movements, and continue to shape the policy goals and aspirations of liberals today. In this section, we will discuss the foundational values and principles that underpin the liberal agenda, such as equality, justice, individual freedom, and social responsibility.

Equality

One of the central tenets of liberalism is the belief in equality, both in terms of rights and opportunities. This principle is rooted in the conviction that all individuals, regardless of race, gender, religion, or socio-economic background, should be treated fairly and have access to the same opportunities for success and well-being. The pursuit of equality has informed a range of policy goals and initiatives within the liberal agenda, from the fight for civil rights and women's suffrage to the push for LGBTQ+ rights and equal pay.

Over time, the concept of equality has evolved to encompass not only formal legal equality but also substantive equality – the idea that sometimes, additional measures are needed to level the playing field for historically marginalized groups. This has given rise to policies such as affirmative action, which seeks to address past discrimination and promote diversity in educational and employment settings.

Justice

Justice is another fundamental principle of liberalism, encompassing both social justice and criminal justice. Social justice refers to the pursuit of a more equitable society, where wealth, power, and opportunities are distributed more fairly, and where the most vulnerable and marginalized members of society are protected and supported. This concept has driven liberals to advocate for policies such as progressive taxation, a robust social safety net, and criminal justice reform.

Criminal justice, on the other hand, focuses on ensuring fairness and due process within the legal system. Liberals have long been concerned with issues such as mass incarceration, racial disparities in sentencing, and police misconduct, and have sought to address these challenges through policy reform and advocacy.

Individual Freedom

The protection of individual freedom is a key value within the liberal tradition, stemming from the belief that individuals should be free to make their own choices and pursue their own goals, so long as they do not infringe upon the rights of others. This principle has informed various aspects of the liberal agenda, from defending the right to free speech and assembly to advocating for reproductive rights and marriage equality.

However, the concept of individual freedom has also evolved over time, with many liberals now recognizing that true freedom is not merely the absence of government intervention but also the presence of the necessary resources and opportunities for individuals to thrive. This has led to an increased focus on policies that seek to remove barriers to success and promote social mobility, such as access to affordable healthcare, education, and housing.

Social Responsibility

Closely related to the values of equality and justice, social responsibility is the belief that individuals and institutions, both public and private, have an obligation to contribute to the well-being of society. This principle underlies many of the policy goals pursued by liberals, such as environmental protection, corporate regulation, and the provision of public goods and services.

In recent years, the concept of social responsibility has also come to encompass the idea of global responsibility, recognizing that the challenges faced by humanity in the 21st century, such as climate change, infectious diseases, and economic inequality, require collective action and cooperation on an international scale.

The core values and principles of modern American liberals – equality, justice, individual freedom, and social responsibility – provide the foundation for the diverse range of policy goals and initiatives pursued by liberals today. While these values have evolved and expanded over time in response to historical events and social movements, they remain central to the liberal agenda, informing its aspirations for a more just, equitable, and inclusive society.

As we navigate the complex challenges of the 21st century, these values and principles continue to guide the liberal movement in its efforts to address issues such as climate change, income inequality, access to affordable healthcare and education, and the protection of civil rights for all Americans. In doing so, liberals seek to strike a balance between individual freedom and the collective good, recognizing that the well-being of society as a whole is inextricably linked to the well-being of each of its members.

By grounding their policy goals in these foundational values and principles, liberals aim to create a society in which everyone has the opportunity to succeed and flourish, regardless of their background or circumstances. Through their commitment to equality, justice, individual freedom, and social responsibility, liberals strive to build a more compassionate and inclusive nation, capable of meeting the challenges of the modern world while remaining true to its democratic ideals.

In the chapters that follow, we will explore in greater detail how these values and principles inform the various policy goals and initiatives pursued by modern American liberals, from addressing economic inequality and promoting social justice to tackling climate change and ensuring equal rights for all citizens. By examining the liberal agenda through the lens of these foundational values, we can gain a deeper understanding of the motivations and aspirations that drive the liberal movement in the United States today.

2: Key Policy Goals and Initiatives of the Modern Liberal Agenda

As we navigate the complexities of these policy goals and initiatives, it is important to remember that the liberal agenda is not monolithic, and there is often a diversity of opinions and approaches within the liberal movement. Nevertheless, the policies discussed in this chapter represent some of the central tenets and aspirations of modern American liberals, and serve as a roadmap for their vision of a more just and equitable society.

2.1: Economic Equality and Social Mobility

One of the key policy goals of the modern liberal agenda is to promote economic equality and social mobility, ensuring that all Americans have the opportunity to succeed and achieve their full potential. In this section, we will examine the various policy initiatives that liberals have proposed to address the challenges of economic inequality and limited social mobility, including progressive taxation, minimum wage increases, and investment in education and job training programs.

Progressive Taxation

A cornerstone of the liberal approach to economic equality is the belief in progressive taxation, which entails a higher tax rate for individuals and corporations with higher incomes. The rationale behind progressive taxation is that those with greater resources should contribute more to the public good, helping to fund essential programs and services that benefit all members of society.

Liberals argue that progressive taxation not only promotes economic fairness but also helps to reduce income inequality by redistributing wealth more evenly across society. In recent years, this has led to calls for reforms such as closing tax loopholes, implementing a wealth tax on the ultra-rich, and increasing the marginal tax rates on the highest income earners.

Minimum Wage Increases

Another key policy initiative aimed at promoting economic equality and social mobility is the push for increases in the minimum wage. Liberals argue that a living wage is essential to ensuring that workers can support themselves and their families, reducing the need for government assistance and enabling greater economic independence.

Over the past several years, there has been a growing movement to raise the federal minimum wage to $15 per hour, with several states and cities already adopting this higher wage standard. Advocates argue that a higher minimum wage not only benefits low-wage workers but also stimulates economic growth by increasing consumer spending and reducing employee turnover.

Investment in Education and Job Training Programs

Access to quality education and job training programs is a crucial aspect of the liberal approach to promoting social mobility. By investing in education, liberals aim to provide individuals with the skills and knowledge necessary to compete in the modern workforce, breaking the cycle of intergenerational poverty and fostering greater economic opportunity.

Key policy initiatives in this area include expanding access to early childhood education, increasing funding for K-12 public schools, and making higher education more affordable through tuition-free community college and income-based student loan repayment programs. In addition, liberals advocate for investment in job training and workforce development programs, particularly in high-demand industries such as healthcare, clean energy, and technology.

The liberal approach to promoting economic equality and social mobility is multifaceted, encompassing a range of policy initiatives designed to level the playing field and create opportunities for all Americans to succeed. Through progressive taxation, minimum wage increases, and investment in education and job training programs, liberals aim to address the systemic barriers that perpetuate economic inequality and limit social mobility.

By pursuing these policy goals, liberals seek to create a more just and equitable society, in which all individuals have the resources and opportunities necessary to achieve their full potential, regardless of their background or circumstances. In the following sections, we will continue to explore the key policy goals and initiatives of the modern liberal agenda, focusing on issues such as healthcare, social welfare, and environmental sustainability.

2.2: Healthcare and Social Welfare

A central focus of the modern liberal agenda is the commitment to ensuring access to affordable healthcare and a robust social safety net for all Americans. In this section, we will explore the various policies and initiatives that liberals have championed in the realms of healthcare and social welfare, including the Affordable Care Act, the expansion of Medicaid, and the push for universal healthcare coverage.

The Affordable Care Act (ACA)

Passed in 2010, the Affordable Care Act (ACA), also known as Obamacare, represented a significant step forward in the liberal quest to expand access to affordable healthcare in the United States. The ACA introduced a variety of reforms aimed at improving the accessibility, affordability, and quality of health insurance, including the creation of health insurance marketplaces, the expansion of Medicaid, and the prohibition of discriminatory practices by insurers, such as denying coverage based on pre-existing conditions.

Despite facing numerous challenges and attempts at repeal, the ACA has resulted in millions of previously uninsured Americans gaining health coverage, and has contributed to a decline in the overall uninsured rate. Liberals continue to advocate for the strengthening and improvement of the ACA, addressing issues such as rising premiums and the stability of the health insurance marketplaces.

Medicaid Expansion

One of the key provisions of the ACA was the expansion of Medicaid, the government health insurance program for low-income individuals and families. The expansion aimed to extend Medicaid coverage to millions of additional Americans who fell into the so-called "coverage gap," earning too much to qualify for traditional Medicaid but too little to afford private insurance.

While many states have opted to expand their Medicaid programs under the ACA, several have not, leaving millions of individuals without access to affordable healthcare coverage. Liberals argue that expanding Medicaid is not only a moral imperative but also an economically sound decision, as it can help to reduce healthcare costs, improve public health outcomes, and stimulate economic growth.

The Push for Universal Healthcare Coverage

Despite the gains made under the ACA, millions of Americans still remain without health insurance, and many others face high out-of-pocket costs and limited access to care. This has led to a growing movement within the liberal camp for the implementation of a universal healthcare system, in which all Americans would have access to comprehensive healthcare coverage, regardless of their income or employment status.

Various models have been proposed for achieving universal healthcare coverage, including a single-payer system, often referred to as "Medicare-for-all," and a public option, which would allow individuals to choose between private insurance and a government-run plan. Advocates argue that universal healthcare would not only ensure access to care for all Americans but could also help to control healthcare costs by reducing administrative expenses and leveraging the government's bargaining power to negotiate lower prices for services and medications.

President Obama was not the first President to push the idea for a Medicare-for-all option. President Clinton pushed for a similar plan in the 1990s. But, another little known plan was started by President Truman in November, 1945. In this plan, Truman explained that because of inadequacies in medical care, many men who were drafted were later found to be unable to serve in WWII due to 4F status. Truman went on to say that if these people received proper medical care, the war would have ended much sooner. Congress ignored him.

The liberal commitment to ensuring access to affordable healthcare and a robust social safety net is a core component of the modern liberal agenda. Through policies such as the ACA, Medicaid expansion, and the push for universal healthcare coverage, liberals seek to create a more compassionate and equitable society in which all Americans have the opportunity to live healthy and secure lives.

In the next section, we will continue our exploration of the key policy goals and initiatives of the modern liberal agenda, focusing on the critical issue of environmental sustainability and climate change.

2.3: Environmental Sustainability and Climate Change

In the face of mounting evidence on the devastating impacts of climate change and environmental degradation, the modern liberal agenda places significant emphasis on promoting environmental sustainability and combating climate change. In this section, we will delve into the various policy proposals and initiatives championed by liberals in the United States, including the Green New Deal, clean energy initiatives, and international cooperation on climate action.

The Green New Deal

The Green New Deal is a comprehensive policy proposal that seeks to address the intertwined challenges of climate change, economic inequality, and social injustice. While not a single piece of legislation, the Green New Deal serves as a broad framework that outlines a series of ambitious goals and policy initiatives aimed at transforming the U.S. economy and achieving net-zero greenhouse gas emissions by 2050.

Key elements of the Green New Deal include transitioning to 100% clean and renewable energy, investing in green infrastructure and public transportation, promoting sustainable agriculture and land use practices, and creating millions of well-paying, green jobs. Additionally, the Green New Deal emphasizes the need for a just transition, ensuring that marginalized communities and workers in the fossil fuel industry are not left behind in the shift to a clean energy economy.

Clean Energy Initiatives

Beyond the Green New Deal, liberals advocate for a range of policies and initiatives aimed at promoting the transition to a clean energy economy. These include increasing investments in renewable energy research and development, providing tax incentives for clean energy production and energy efficiency improvements, and implementing renewable energy standards and carbon pricing mechanisms to reduce greenhouse gas emissions.

Furthermore, liberals emphasize the importance of investing in the modernization and expansion of the electric grid, as well as the development of energy storage technologies, to accommodate the increased integration of renewable energy sources. By supporting the growth of the clean energy sector, liberals aim to create new economic opportunities, enhance energy security, and reduce the nation's reliance on fossil fuels.

International Cooperation on Climate Action

Recognizing that climate change is a global challenge that requires coordinated action, liberals advocate for strong international cooperation on climate action. This includes recommitting to and strengthening the Paris Agreement, a landmark international accord that sets forth a framework for countries to reduce their greenhouse gas emissions and mitigate the impacts of climate change.

Liberals also stress the importance of providing financial and technical assistance to developing countries to support their transition to clean energy and build resilience to climate impacts. By engaging in global climate diplomacy and supporting multilateral efforts to combat climate change, liberals seek to reaffirm the United States' commitment to addressing this existential threat and to demonstrate leadership on the world stage.

The liberal agenda's focus on environmental sustainability and climate change reflects a deep-seated recognition of the urgent need to protect the planet for future generations and to address the social and economic disparities that are exacerbated by environmental degradation. Through policy proposals such as the Green New Deal, clean energy initiatives, and international cooperation on climate action, liberals strive to create a more sustainable, equitable, and resilient society capable of meeting the challenges of the 21st century.

By examining the key policy goals and initiatives of the modern liberal agenda, we have gained a deeper understanding of the values, principles, and aspirations that underpin the liberal movement in the United States today. As we continue to confront the complex and interrelated challenges of our time, the liberal agenda offers a vision of a more just, inclusive, and sustainable society in which all Americans have the opportunity to thrive and succeed.

3: Universal Healthcare

One of the most prominent and passionately debated goals within the modern liberal agenda is the pursuit of universal healthcare coverage in the United States. The vision of a society in which all citizens have access to affordable, high-quality healthcare, regardless of their income or employment status, is deeply rooted in the liberal principles of equality, justice, and social responsibility.

As we navigate the intricacies of this critical issue, it is important to remember that the debate surrounding universal healthcare is not solely a matter of policy or economics, but also one of ethics and values. At its core, the push for universal healthcare reflects a deep-seated belief in the fundamental right to health and well-being, and the moral imperative to ensure that all Americans have the opportunity to live healthy, fulfilling lives.

3.1: The Case for Universal Healthcare

The push for universal healthcare in the United States is driven by a variety of compelling arguments that emphasize the potential benefits of such a system, not only for individuals but also for society as a whole. In this section, we will outline the main arguments in favor of universal healthcare, focusing on its potential to increase access to care, improve health outcomes, reduce healthcare costs, and promote greater health equity among different segments of the population.

Increased Access to Care

One of the primary arguments for universal healthcare is that it would significantly increase access to healthcare services for millions of Americans who are currently uninsured or underinsured. By removing financial barriers to care, such as high premiums, deductibles, and copayments, universal healthcare would enable more people to seek timely medical attention and preventive services, thereby improving overall health and well-being.

Improved Health Outcomes

Research has consistently shown that individuals with health insurance tend to have better health outcomes than those without coverage. By providing comprehensive healthcare coverage to all Americans, universal healthcare has the potential to improve population health by increasing the utilization of preventive services, facilitating early detection and treatment of illnesses, and reducing the prevalence of chronic conditions.

Reduced Healthcare Costs

Another major argument in favor of universal healthcare is its potential to reduce overall healthcare costs. By consolidating the healthcare system under a single payer, administrative inefficiencies and redundancies could be significantly reduced, leading to cost savings. Additionally, a single-payer system would have greater bargaining power to negotiate lower prices for medical services and prescription drugs, further driving down costs.

Moreover, by increasing access to preventive care and early intervention, universal healthcare could help to reduce the burden of expensive emergency care and hospitalizations, resulting in additional cost savings. Some estimates suggest that a single-payer healthcare system could save the United States hundreds of billions of dollars annually.

Promotion of Health Equity

The current healthcare system in the United States is characterized by significant disparities in access to care and health outcomes among different racial, ethnic, and socioeconomic groups. Universal healthcare has the potential to promote greater health equity by ensuring that all Americans have access to high-quality healthcare services, regardless of their background or financial resources.

By eliminating financial barriers to care and providing comprehensive coverage, universal healthcare could help to reduce disparities in health outcomes, preventable deaths, and chronic disease prevalence among historically underserved populations.

The case for universal healthcare in the United States is rooted in a diverse array of arguments that emphasize its potential to improve access to care, enhance health outcomes, reduce healthcare costs, and promote greater health equity. While the path to achieving universal healthcare is fraught with challenges and obstacles, the potential benefits of such a system offer a compelling vision of a more just, equitable, and healthy society.

3.2: Policy Proposals for Achieving Universal Healthcare

To achieve the goal of universal healthcare coverage in the United States, liberals have put forth a range of policy proposals that seek to build upon and expand the existing healthcare infrastructure. These proposals can be broadly classified into three main categories: the single-payer "Medicare-for-all" system, the public option, and the expansion of existing programs like Medicaid. In this section, we will discuss each of these policy proposals in detail, highlighting their key features, strengths, and potential drawbacks.

Single-Payer "Medicare-for-all" System

The most ambitious and comprehensive policy proposal for achieving universal healthcare is the single-payer "Medicare-for-all" system, which envisions a complete overhaul of the current healthcare system in favor of a centralized, government-run program that would provide healthcare coverage to all Americans.

Under a "Medicare-for-all" system, all U.S. residents would be automatically enrolled in a single, national health insurance program, which would replace private insurance, employer-sponsored coverage, and most existing public programs. The government would serve as the sole payer for healthcare services, covering a comprehensive range of benefits, including primary care, hospital care, prescription drugs, dental and vision care, and long-term care.

The "Medicare-for-all" proposal has several notable strengths, including its potential to significantly increase access to care, simplify the healthcare system, reduce administrative costs, and promote health equity. However, it also faces several challenges, such as the need for substantial tax increases to fund the program, potential opposition from the private insurance industry and other stakeholders, and concerns about the feasibility of implementing such a sweeping reform.

Public Option

Another policy proposal for achieving universal healthcare is the creation of a public option, which would involve the establishment of a government-run health insurance plan that would compete with private insurers in the healthcare marketplace. The public option would be available to all Americans, regardless of their income or employment status, and would provide comprehensive healthcare coverage at affordable rates.

The public option aims to increase competition in the healthcare market, potentially driving down premiums and improving the quality of care. By offering an affordable alternative to private insurance, the public option could help to expand coverage to millions of uninsured and underinsured Americans.

However, the public option also faces several challenges, such as the need to ensure that the government plan can compete effectively with private insurers, potential resistance from stakeholders in the healthcare industry, and concerns about the long-term financial sustainability of the program.

Expansion of Existing Programs

A third approach to achieving universal healthcare involves the expansion of existing public programs, such as Medicaid and the Children's Health Insurance Program (CHIP). This could be accomplished by increasing eligibility thresholds, streamlining enrollment processes, and providing additional funding to states to support the expansion of coverage.

By building on the existing infrastructure of public healthcare programs, this approach offers a more incremental path to achieving universal healthcare coverage. However, it may not address some of the fundamental challenges facing the U.S. healthcare system, such as high costs, administrative inefficiencies, and fragmentation of care.

The policy proposals put forth by liberals to achieve universal healthcare coverage in the United States reflect a diverse range of approaches, each with its own unique strengths and challenges. While there is no one-size-fits-all solution to the complex issue of healthcare reform, these proposals offer a starting point for a meaningful and constructive dialogue about how best to ensure that all Americans have access to affordable, high-quality healthcare.

In the next section, we will delve deeper into the benefits and challenges associated with implementing a single-payer healthcare system, which represents the most ambitious and far-reaching of the policy proposals discussed in this section.

3.3: Benefits and Challenges of a Single-Payer Healthcare System

A single-payer healthcare system represents the most comprehensive and transformative approach to achieving universal healthcare coverage in the United States. While this ambitious proposal offers numerous potential benefits, it also faces significant challenges and obstacles that must be carefully considered and addressed. In this section, we provide an in-depth analysis of the benefits and challenges associated with implementing a single-payer healthcare system, focusing on its potential impacts on healthcare access, quality, cost, and the broader economy, as well as the political and logistical hurdles that must be overcome to realize this goal.

Benefits of a Single-Payer Healthcare System

1. Improved Access to Care: By providing comprehensive healthcare coverage to all Americans, a single-payer system would eliminate financial barriers to care and significantly increase access to medical services for millions of uninsured and underinsured individuals.
2. Enhanced Health Outcomes: With greater access to preventive services, early intervention, and timely treatment, a single-payer system could lead to improved health outcomes for the population as a whole, reducing the burden of chronic diseases and preventable deaths.
3. Cost Savings and Efficiency: A single-payer system would streamline healthcare administration, reducing redundancies and inefficiencies that contribute to high healthcare costs. Additionally, the government would have greater negotiating power to secure lower prices for medical services and prescription drugs, further reducing overall healthcare spending.
4. Health Equity: By ensuring that all Americans have access to high-quality healthcare services, regardless of their income, employment status, or background, a single-payer system would promote greater health equity and reduce disparities in health outcomes among different segments of the population.

Challenges of a Single-Payer Healthcare System

1. Funding: Implementing a single-payer healthcare system would require significant public investment, which would likely necessitate tax increases or reallocation of resources from other areas of the federal budget. The potential impact on taxpayers and the economy is a major concern for opponents of the single-payer system.
2. Transition and Disruption: Transitioning to a single-payer system would involve a major overhaul of the existing healthcare infrastructure, which could cause disruption for patients, providers, and other stakeholders. The logistical challenges of implementing such a sweeping reform would be considerable and could generate resistance from various quarters.
3. Potential Impact on Quality and Innovation: Critics of a single-payer system argue that government control of healthcare could lead to reduced quality of care, as providers may have less incentive to innovate or invest in new technologies and treatments. However, proponents argue that a single-payer system would allow for more equitable allocation of resources and a focus on value-based care.
4. Political Resistance: Achieving the political consensus necessary to implement a single-payer healthcare system is a major challenge, given the significant opposition from various stakeholders, including the private insurance industry, healthcare providers, and conservative politicians. Overcoming these political hurdles would require a sustained and concerted effort by supporters of the single-payer system.

The benefits and challenges associated with implementing a single-payer healthcare system in the United States highlight the complexities and trade-offs inherent in the pursuit of universal healthcare coverage. While a single-payer system offers the potential for significant improvements in access to care, health outcomes, and cost savings, it also faces numerous obstacles that must be carefully navigated and addressed.

As the debate over healthcare reform continues to unfold, it is essential for policymakers, healthcare providers, and the public to engage in a thoughtful and informed dialogue about the best path forward to ensure that all Americans have access to affordable, high-quality healthcare. Ultimately, the success of any healthcare reform effort will depend on the ability to balance competing interests, overcome logistical and political barriers, and adapt to the ever-evolving needs and demands of the U.S. healthcare system.

4: Income Inequality and Wealth Redistribution

Income inequality and wealth redistribution are central concerns for liberals in the United States, as they seek to address the growing wealth disparities that have emerged over the past several decades. These disparities have far-reaching consequences, affecting not only individual well-being but also the overall health and stability of the nation's economy and social fabric. In this chapter, we will explore the liberal perspective on income inequality and wealth redistribution, examining the various policy initiatives and measures that have been proposed to tackle this complex and pressing issue.

4.1: The Growing Problem of Income Inequality

Income inequality has been a growing concern in the United States, as the gap between the rich and the poor continues to widen at an alarming rate. In this section, we will delve into the issue of income inequality, exploring its historical development, current trends, and the consequences of widening wealth disparities for individuals and society as a whole.

Historical Development of Income Inequality in the United States

Income inequality has been a persistent feature of American society, but its severity has fluctuated over time. In the early 20th century, the United States experienced a period of extreme income inequality, which peaked during the 1920s. However, the Great Depression, followed by the New Deal and the post-World War II economic boom, led to a significant reduction in income disparities, as progressive taxation, labor protections, and social welfare programs were implemented.

From the 1940s to the 1970s, the United States enjoyed a period of relative economic equality, known as the "Great Compression." However, since the late 1970s, income inequality has been on the rise again, driven by factors such as globalization, technological change, the decline of labor unions, and changes in tax and regulatory policies that disproportionately benefit the wealthy.

Current Trends in Income Inequality

Today, income inequality in the United States has reached levels not seen since the early 20th century. The richest 1% of Americans now hold a greater share of the nation's wealth than the bottom 90% combined. Over the past four decades, the real incomes of the top 1% have grown by more than 200%, while the real incomes of the bottom 50% have barely increased at all.

These trends have been exacerbated by the Great Recession of 2007-2009, which disproportionately impacted low-income and middle-class households, leading to a further concentration of wealth among the richest Americans. Despite recent economic growth, the recovery has been uneven, with wages for the majority of workers remaining stagnant while corporate profits and executive compensation continue to soar.

Consequences of Widening Wealth Disparities

The consequences of rising income inequality are far-reaching, affecting not only the well-being of individuals but also the overall health and stability of society. Some of the key consequences of widening wealth disparities include:

1. Reduced Economic Growth: High levels of income inequality can undermine economic growth, as lower- and middle-class households have less disposable income to spend on goods and services. This, in turn, can lead to reduced demand, lower business investment, and slower job creation.
2. Weaker Social Mobility: Income inequality can limit opportunities for social mobility, making it more difficult for individuals from lower-income backgrounds to move up the economic ladder. This can result in a society where one's

economic prospects are largely determined by the circumstances of their birth, rather than their talent and hard work.

3. Increased Poverty and Economic Hardship: As wealth becomes concentrated among a smaller share of the population, more individuals and families may struggle to make ends meet, leading to higher levels of poverty and economic hardship.

4. Erosion of Social Cohesion and Trust: Widening wealth disparities can contribute to an erosion of social cohesion and trust, as individuals become increasingly divided along economic lines. This can lead to increased social tensions, political polarization, and a weakening of the social fabric that underpins a healthy democracy.

In the next sections, we will explore the policy solutions proposed by liberals to address the growing problem of income inequality in the United States, focusing on progressive taxation, wealth redistribution policies, and measures to promote economic mobility and social welfare.

4.2: Progressive Taxation and Wealth Redistribution Policies

One of the key strategies embraced by liberals to address income inequality is the implementation of progressive taxation and wealth redistribution policies. These policies aim to ensure that those with higher incomes and wealth contribute a greater share of their resources to the public good, helping to fund social programs and public services that benefit society as a whole. In this section, we will discuss some of the main policy proposals put forth by liberals to address income inequality through progressive taxation and wealth redistribution.

Higher Tax Rates for Top Earners

A central tenet of the liberal approach to taxation is the belief that those with higher incomes should be taxed at higher rates. This principle is based on the idea of "vertical equity," which holds that individuals with greater financial resources have a greater ability to contribute to the public good. By taxing top earners at higher rates, liberals argue that the government can generate additional revenue to fund social programs, infrastructure investments, and other public services that benefit all citizens, while also reducing income inequality.

Various proposals have been put forth to increase tax rates for top earners, such as raising the top marginal income tax rate or implementing a more progressive tax structure. Some liberals also advocate for the reintroduction of higher tax brackets for the ultra-wealthy, which were more prevalent in the past. For example, during the 1950s and 1960s, the top marginal income tax rate in the United States exceeded 90% for the highest earners.

Wealth Taxes

In addition to progressive income taxation, some liberals argue that wealth taxes should be implemented to help address income inequality. A wealth tax is a levy on the total value of an individual's net worth, rather than their income. Proponents of wealth taxes contend that they can help to reduce the concentration of wealth among the richest Americans, while generating substantial revenue to fund social programs and public services.

One prominent proposal for a wealth tax in the United States is the "Ultra-Millionaire Tax" put forth by Senator Elizabeth Warren, which would impose a 2% annual tax on households with a net worth between $50 million and $1 billion, and a 3% tax on households with a net worth above $1 billion. Critics of wealth taxes argue that they can be difficult to administer and enforce, may encourage tax avoidance, and could potentially discourage investment and economic growth.

Closing Tax Loopholes that Benefit the Wealthy

Another key component of the liberal approach to addressing income inequality through taxation is the push to close tax loopholes that disproportionately benefit the wealthy. Examples of such loopholes include the preferential tax treatment of capital gains and dividends, the carried interest loophole, and various deductions and credits that are primarily utilized by high-income individuals and corporations.

By closing these loopholes and ensuring that the tax code is more equitable, liberals argue that the government can generate additional revenue to fund public services and social programs, while also reducing income inequality by requiring the wealthy to pay their fair share of taxes.

The liberal approach to addressing income inequality through progressive taxation and wealth redistribution policies involves a range of measures, including higher tax rates for top earners, the implementation of wealth taxes, and the closing of tax loopholes that disproportionately benefit the wealthy. These policies aim to create a more equitable society by ensuring that those with greater financial resources contribute a larger share of their wealth to the public good, while also providing the necessary funding for social programs and public services that benefit all citizens.

4.3: Minimum Wage, Social Welfare, and Economic Mobility

In addition to progressive taxation and wealth redistribution policies, liberals also advocate for a range of other measures aimed at promoting economic mobility, reducing income inequality, and providing a safety net for vulnerable citizens. In this section, we will explore some of these policies, focusing on raising the minimum wage, strengthening social welfare programs, and investing in education and job training.

Raising the Minimum Wage

One of the key policy proposals put forth by liberals to address income inequality is the call to raise the minimum wage. The minimum wage is the lowest hourly wage that employers are legally required to pay their workers, and it serves as a basic floor for labor market compensation. Advocates for raising the minimum wage argue that doing so can help to lift millions of workers out of poverty, reduce income inequality, and stimulate economic growth by increasing the purchasing power of low-wage workers.

Several proposals have been made to raise the federal minimum wage in the United States, such as the "Fight for $15" movement, which seeks to gradually increase the minimum wage to $15 per hour. Some states and cities have already enacted laws to raise their minimum wages above the current federal level of $7.25 per hour. Critics of raising the minimum wage argue that it could lead to job losses, as employers may be forced to cut hours or positions in response to higher labor costs.

Strengthening Social Welfare Programs

Another important aspect of the liberal approach to addressing income inequality and promoting economic mobility is the call to strengthen social welfare programs. These programs, which include unemployment insurance, food assistance, housing subsidies, and cash transfers, provide a crucial safety net for individuals and families who are struggling to make ends meet.

Liberals argue that by expanding and improving social welfare programs, the government can help to alleviate poverty, reduce income inequality, and ensure that all citizens have access to basic necessities such as food, housing, and healthcare. Some specific proposals include increasing the generosity of programs like the Earned Income Tax Credit and the Supplemental Nutrition Assistance Program (SNAP), expanding access to affordable housing, and modernizing the unemployment insurance system to better serve workers in today's economy.

Investing in Education and Job Training

Finally, liberals contend that investing in education and job training is essential for promoting economic mobility and reducing income inequality. By ensuring that all citizens have access to high-quality education and the skills needed to succeed in the modern labor market, the government can help to level the playing field and create more equitable opportunities for economic advancement.

Specific proposals for investing in education and job training include expanding access to early childhood education, increasing funding for K-12 public schools, making college more affordable through grants and low-interest loans, and supporting job training programs for adults, particularly in industries that are experiencing rapid technological change.

The liberal approach to addressing income inequality and promoting economic mobility involves a combination of policy measures, including raising the minimum wage, strengthening social welfare programs, and investing in education and job training. These policies aim to provide a safety net for vulnerable citizens, while also creating the conditions for greater economic opportunity and a more equitable distribution of wealth and resources in society.

5: Education Reform and Accessibility

Education is a cornerstone of the liberal agenda, as it is widely recognized as a critical driver of social mobility, economic prosperity, and personal fulfillment. In this chapter, we will examine the liberal vision for education reform, focusing on increasing accessibility to quality education for all Americans, reducing the achievement gap, and promoting policies such as universal pre-K and affordable higher education.

Liberals believe that a well-funded and equitable public education system is essential to ensuring that every child, regardless of their background, has the opportunity to succeed in life. To achieve this vision, they advocate for a range of policies aimed at addressing the various barriers that prevent many students from accessing high-quality education, from socioeconomic disparities and unequal funding to outdated curricula and inadequate support for teachers. By implementing these reforms, liberals hope to create a more inclusive and effective education system that better serves the diverse needs of America's students and prepares them for the challenges of the 21st century.

5.1: Universal Pre-K and Early Childhood Education

Early childhood education has increasingly become a focus for liberals, as a growing body of research underscores the importance of these formative years in shaping children's cognitive development, school readiness, and long-term educational outcomes. In this section, we will explore the push for implementing universal pre-K programs and the potential benefits of investing in early childhood education.

The Importance of Early Childhood Education

Early childhood education encompasses the learning experiences that children receive from birth to age five, a critical period in which the foundation for lifelong learning, socio-emotional skills, and cognitive development is laid. Research has demonstrated that high-quality early childhood education programs can have a profound impact on a child's future success, leading to improved academic performance, reduced rates of grade repetition and special education placements, and higher rates of high school graduation and college enrollment.

The Liberal Push for Universal Pre-K

Recognizing the importance of early childhood education, liberals have increasingly advocated for the implementation of universal pre-K programs, which would provide all children with access to high-quality preschool education, regardless of their families' income levels or geographic location. These programs aim to level the playing field for children from disadvantaged backgrounds, who often enter kindergarten with significant gaps in cognitive development and school readiness compared to their more affluent peers.

Potential Benefits of Universal Pre-K Programs

The potential benefits of implementing universal pre-K programs are numerous and far-reaching. First and foremost, these programs can help to narrow the achievement gap between children from different socioeconomic backgrounds, as they ensure that all children have access to the high-quality early learning experiences that are crucial for cognitive development and school readiness. This, in turn, can lead to more equitable educational outcomes throughout K-12 education and beyond.

Second, universal pre-K programs have been shown to generate long-term economic benefits, as they lead to higher levels of educational attainment, increased workforce productivity, and reduced social costs associated with crime, unemployment, and dependence on public assistance. By investing in early childhood education, the government can lay the groundwork for a more prosperous and equitable society in the long run.

Last, universal pre-K programs can also have positive spillover effects on families and communities, as they provide parents with access to affordable childcare, promote parental involvement in their children's education, and foster a culture of lifelong learning.

The liberal push for implementing universal pre-K programs reflects a growing recognition of the importance of early childhood education in shaping children's cognitive development, school readiness, and long-term educational outcomes. By investing in high-quality preschool education for all children, regardless of their background, liberals hope to create a more equitable and effective education system that better serves the diverse needs of America's students and prepares them for the challenges of the 21st century.

5.2: K-12 Education Reform and Reducing the Achievement Gap

Addressing the myriad challenges facing the K-12 education system is a top priority for liberals, who recognize that an effective and equitable public education system is essential for promoting social mobility and ensuring the long-term success of America's diverse student population. In this section, we will delve into the various policy proposals put forth by liberals to reform K-12 education, with an emphasis on reducing the achievement gap between students from different socioeconomic backgrounds, improving educational equity, and enhancing the overall quality of public education.

Addressing Funding Inequities

One of the central challenges facing the American education system is the persistent funding disparities that exist between schools in wealthy and low-income communities. These funding inequities, which are largely driven by the reliance on local property taxes to finance public education, contribute to a wide range of educational disparities, including unequal access to experienced teachers, advanced coursework, and extracurricular activities.

To address this issue, liberals advocate for a more equitable distribution of education funding, with increased support for schools in low-income areas. This may involve implementing progressive funding formulas that allocate more resources to schools with higher concentrations of disadvantaged students, as well as providing targeted grants for specific purposes, such as hiring more experienced teachers or expanding access to advanced courses.

Improving Teacher Quality and Support

Research has consistently shown that teacher quality is one of the most important factors influencing student achievement. However, many schools, particularly those serving low-income communities, struggle to attract and retain experienced and effective educators. To address this challenge, liberals propose a range of policies aimed at improving teacher quality and support, such as offering competitive salaries, providing ongoing professional development opportunities, and creating mentorship programs for new teachers. Additionally, they advocate for measures to increase the diversity of the teaching workforce, as research has shown that students of color often benefit from having teachers who share their racial and cultural background.

Promoting Student-Centered Learning

Liberals also emphasize the importance of implementing student-centered learning approaches that cater to the diverse needs and interests of America's students. This includes promoting differentiated instruction, project-based learning, and culturally responsive teaching practices that engage and empower students from all backgrounds. In addition, they support the expansion of personalized learning initiatives that leverage technology to provide students with customized learning experiences tailored to their unique strengths, needs, and learning styles.

Expanding Access to High-Quality Curriculum and Resources

Another key aspect of the liberal approach to K-12 education reform is ensuring that all students have access to high-quality curriculum and resources. This includes promoting the adoption of rigorous, research-based standards that prepare students for success in college and the workforce, as well as ensuring that schools are equipped with the necessary textbooks, technology, and other instructional materials. In addition, liberals support efforts to expand access to advanced coursework, such as Advanced Placement and International Baccalaureate programs, as well as enrichment opportunities in the arts, sciences, and other disciplines.

The liberal agenda for K-12 education reform seeks to address the persistent achievement gap between students from different socioeconomic backgrounds by promoting policies that improve educational equity, enhance the quality of public education, and cater to the diverse needs and interests of America's students. Through these efforts, liberals aim to create a more inclusive and effective education system that provides all children with the opportunity to succeed, regardless of their background or circumstances.

5.3: Affordable Higher Education and Workforce Development

As the demands of the 21st-century economy continue to evolve, the need for an educated and skilled workforce has never been greater. To ensure that all Americans have the opportunity to succeed in this rapidly changing landscape, liberals advocate for policies aimed at making higher education more accessible and affordable, as well as promoting workforce development initiatives. In this section, we will discuss the liberal approach to these issues, including increased funding for public colleges and universities, expansion of financial aid programs, and support for vocational education and job training initiatives.

Increased Funding for Public Colleges and Universities

One of the main ways liberals seek to make higher education more accessible and affordable is by increasing funding for public colleges and universities. By investing in these institutions, the government can help to lower tuition costs, expand access to high-quality academic programs, and provide additional support services for students from disadvantaged backgrounds.

Furthermore, increased funding can help to ensure that public institutions have the necessary resources to recruit and retain top-tier faculty, maintain state-of-the-art facilities, and conduct cutting-edge research.

Expansion of Financial Aid Programs

In addition to increased funding for public institutions, liberals also advocate for the expansion of financial aid programs that help to reduce the financial burden on students and their families. This includes supporting policies such as increasing the maximum Pell Grant award, creating more generous income-based repayment plans for federal student loans, and expanding access to tuition-free community college programs. By making higher education more affordable, these policies can help to reduce the financial barriers that often prevent low-income students from pursuing a college degree.

Some states are investigating subsidizing college tuition, much like North Carolina's NC Promise program in which three universities have subsidized tuition at $500 per semester.

Support for Vocational Education and Job Training Initiatives

Recognizing that not all students are interested in or best served by a traditional four-year college degree, liberals also emphasize the importance of promoting vocational education and job training initiatives. These programs, which provide students with the skills and credentials needed to enter high-demand industries such as healthcare, technology, and advanced manufacturing, can play a critical role in preparing America's workforce for the jobs of the future.

To support these initiatives, liberals advocate for policies such as increased funding for career and technical education (CTE) programs, the creation of apprenticeship opportunities in partnership with industry, and the expansion of access to short-term credential programs that provide targeted training in specific skills. By investing in these alternative pathways to career success, liberals aim to ensure that all Americans have the opportunity to acquire the skills and knowledge needed to thrive in the 21st-century economy.

The liberal approach to affordable higher education and workforce development seeks to ensure that all Americans have the opportunity to acquire the skills, knowledge, and credentials needed to succeed in the modern economy. By increasing funding for public colleges and universities, expanding financial aid programs, and promoting vocational education and job training initiatives, liberals aim to create a more inclusive and accessible higher education system that better serves the diverse needs and aspirations of America's students.

6: Civil Rights and Social Justice

At the core of the liberal agenda is a steadfast commitment to advancing civil rights and promoting social justice for all Americans. This dedication is rooted in the belief that every individual, regardless of race, gender, sexual orientation, or socioeconomic background, deserves equal protection under the law and the opportunity to thrive in a just and inclusive society. In this chapter, we will delve into the various ways in which liberals strive to address systemic discrimination, combat inequality, and promote the rights and well-being of marginalized communities. From LGBTQ+ rights and racial equity to gender equality and women's rights, the liberal approach to civil rights and social justice encompasses a wide range of interconnected issues and policy initiatives aimed at fostering a more equitable and just society for all.

6.1: LGBTQ+ Rights and Equality

The liberal commitment to advancing LGBTQ+ rights and promoting equality for all, regardless of sexual orientation or gender identity, is rooted in the fundamental belief that LGBTQ+ rights are human rights. Recognizing that discrimination, prejudice, and marginalization of LGBTQ+ individuals are not only unjust but also inhumane, liberals work tirelessly to develop policy initiatives aimed at ending discrimination, ensuring legal protections, and promoting inclusivity in various aspects of society.

Ending Discrimination

A key element of the liberal approach to LGBTQ+ rights is the pursuit of policies that explicitly prohibit discrimination based on sexual orientation and gender identity. This includes advocating for the passage of comprehensive non-discrimination laws at the federal, state, and local levels, which would protect LGBTQ+ individuals from discrimination in areas such as employment, housing, public accommodations, and education. By pushing for these protections, liberals aim to ensure that LGBTQ+ individuals can live, work, and learn free from the fear of discrimination and prejudice.

Ensuring Legal Protections

In addition to fighting discrimination, liberals also focus on securing legal protections and rights for LGBTQ+ individuals in other areas of the law. This includes supporting marriage equality, which was affirmed by the Supreme Court in the landmark case of Obergefell v. Hodges in 2015, and advocating for the rights of transgender individuals to access public spaces, such as restrooms, in accordance with their gender identity. Furthermore, liberals have been at the forefront of efforts to ban conversion therapy, a harmful and discredited practice that seeks to change an individual's sexual orientation or gender identity, and to ensure that LGBTQ+ individuals have equal access to healthcare, including gender-affirming care.

Promoting Inclusivity

Beyond policy initiatives aimed at ending discrimination and ensuring legal protections, the liberal commitment to LGBTQ+ rights also encompasses efforts to promote inclusivity and acceptance in various aspects of society. This includes advocating for comprehensive, age-appropriate, and LGBTQ+-inclusive sex education in schools, supporting initiatives that aim to address bullying and harassment of LGBTQ+ students, and pushing for policies that ensure fair treatment and equal opportunities for LGBTQ+ individuals in the workplace. By fostering a culture of inclusivity, liberals seek to create an environment in which LGBTQ+ individuals are not only legally protected but also feel respected, valued, and accepted for who they are.

The liberal commitment to advancing LGBTQ+ rights and promoting equality for all is rooted in the belief that all individuals, regardless of their sexual orientation or gender identity, are entitled to the same rights, protections, and opportunities. By pursuing policy initiatives that end discrimination, ensure legal protections, and promote inclusivity, liberals work to create a society in which LGBTQ+ individuals can live their lives free from prejudice and injustice, and enjoy the same rights and freedoms as any other citizen. In doing so, they reaffirm the fundamental principle that LGBTQ+ rights are indeed human rights, and that it is both inhuman and inhumane to block or otherwise diminish the rights of any group.

6.2: Racial Equity and Criminal Justice Reform

Addressing systemic racism and promoting racial equity are central tenets of the liberal agenda in the United States. Recognizing that racial disparities continue to pervade numerous aspects of society, liberals work to dismantle the structures and policies that perpetuate these inequities. This section delves into the liberal approach to racial equity, focusing on criminal justice reform, police accountability, and measures to reduce racial disparities in areas such as education, housing, and employment.

Criminal Justice Reform

One of the most significant ways in which liberals seek to address systemic racism is through criminal justice reform. The United States has the highest incarceration rate in the world, with a disproportionate number of those incarcerated being people of color, particularly African Americans and Latinos. To combat this, liberals advocate for a range of reforms that include eliminating mandatory minimum sentences for nonviolent drug offenses, reforming the cash bail system, which disproportionately impacts low-income individuals, and promoting the use of alternatives to incarceration, such as drug courts, mental health courts, and restorative justice programs. Additionally, liberals push for the end of the "war on drugs" and the decriminalization or legalization of certain substances, such as marijuana, which have disproportionately impacted communities of color.

Police Accountability

In recent years, the issue of police violence against unarmed people of color has gained national attention, highlighting the urgent need for police accountability and reform. Liberals demand greater transparency, oversight, and accountability within law enforcement agencies.

This includes advocating for the use of body cameras, the establishment of civilian review boards to investigate police misconduct, and the implementation of de-escalation training and other evidence-based practices designed to reduce the use of force. Furthermore, liberals call for reallocating a portion of police budgets towards social services and community-based programs that address the root causes of crime, such as poverty, mental illness, and addiction, which is often referred to as "defunding the police," an unfortunate name for a policy that would help thousands of people who are currently, and potentially heading to, prison.

Reducing Racial Disparities in Education, Housing, and Employment

Beyond the realm of criminal justice, liberals also work to address racial disparities in areas like education, housing, and employment. In education, they advocate for policies that promote diversity and reduce the achievement gap, such as increased funding for low-income schools, universal pre-K programs, and efforts to desegregate schools through redistricting and affirmative action policies. In housing, liberals push for the enforcement of fair housing laws and the implementation of policies that promote affordable housing and combat residential segregation. In employment, they support measures that aim to reduce discrimination in hiring and promote workforce diversity, such as equal pay legislation, affirmative action policies, and targeted workforce development programs.

The liberal approach to addressing systemic racism and promoting racial equity in the United States involves tackling the issue from multiple angles. Through criminal justice reform, police accountability, and targeted measures to reduce racial disparities in areas like education, housing, and employment, liberals strive to create a more equitable and just society in which individuals of all races have equal opportunities to succeed and thrive.

6.3: Gender Equality and Women's Rights

The liberal commitment to advancing gender equality and women's rights is rooted in the belief that all individuals, regardless of their gender, should have equal opportunities and protections under the law. This section examines the various issues that are central to the liberal agenda on gender equality, including equal pay, reproductive rights, and the prevention of gender-based violence. It highlights policy proposals and initiatives aimed at fostering greater gender equity in various aspects of society.

Equal Pay and Workplace Equality

One of the key areas of focus for liberals in their pursuit of gender equality is ensuring equal pay for equal work. Despite progress in recent decades, the gender pay gap persists, with women earning on average only a fraction of what men earn for the same work. Liberals advocate for policies such as the Paycheck Fairness Act, which seeks to strengthen existing equal pay laws and close loopholes that have allowed employers to discriminate based on gender. Additionally, they promote measures to increase transparency around pay, such as requiring employers to disclose salary information for comparable positions, and support efforts to encourage more women to enter higher-paying, male-dominated fields through targeted education and training programs.

Reproductive Rights

The protection and expansion of reproductive rights is another critical aspect of the liberal agenda on gender equality. Liberals firmly believe that every individual should have the right to make decisions about their own reproductive health, including access to safe and legal abortion, affordable contraception, and comprehensive sex education. They oppose efforts to restrict or undermine these rights, such as the defunding of Planned Parenthood or the passage of restrictive abortion laws. Furthermore, liberals advocate for policies that support reproductive justice, such as expanding access to maternal healthcare, addressing racial disparities in maternal mortality rates, and providing paid family leave for all workers.

Prevention of Gender-Based Violence

Liberals are also committed to addressing and preventing gender-based violence, which disproportionately affects women and girls. They support the reauthorization and strengthening of the Violence Against Women Act (VAWA), which provides crucial funding and resources for programs aimed at preventing and responding to domestic violence, sexual assault, and stalking. Additionally, liberals call for increased funding for victim services, the expansion of legal protections for survivors, and the implementation of prevention programs that address the root causes of gender-based violence, such as toxic masculinity and societal norms that perpetuate violence against women.

The liberal commitment to advancing gender equality and women's rights encompasses a wide range of issues, from equal pay and workplace equality to reproductive rights and the prevention of gender-based violence. Through policy proposals and initiatives aimed at fostering greater gender equity in various aspects of society, liberals work to create a more just and equal world in which individuals of all genders have the opportunity to thrive and reach their full potential.

7: Criminal Justice Reform

The United States has the highest incarceration rate in the world, with millions of people behind bars at any given time. This has led to a growing recognition among liberals that the criminal justice system is in dire need of reform. In this chapter, we will explore the liberal agenda for criminal justice reform, with an emphasis on ending mass incarceration, abolishing the death penalty, and promoting community-based alternatives to punishment. We will discuss the various policy proposals and initiatives that liberals advocate for in order to create a more just, humane, and effective system that focuses on rehabilitation, reintegration, and the reduction of recidivism. By addressing the root causes of crime and embracing evidence-based practices, liberals aim to transform the criminal justice system into one that is more equitable and that better serves the needs of individuals, families, and communities across the nation.

7.1: Ending Mass Incarceration and Sentencing Reform

Mass incarceration has become a defining characteristic of the American criminal justice system, with the United States having the highest incarceration rate in the world. This phenomenon has had devastating consequences for individuals, families, and communities, particularly for people of color and those from disadvantaged backgrounds. Recognizing the urgent need for change, liberals have been at the forefront of efforts to reform sentencing practices and reduce the nation's reliance on imprisonment.

One of the key drivers of mass incarceration has been the widespread use of mandatory minimum sentences, which require judges to impose a predetermined minimum prison term for certain offenses, regardless of the individual circumstances of the case. This approach has been criticized for contributing to the dramatic rise in prison populations, as well as for perpetuating racial and socioeconomic disparities within the criminal justice system. In response, liberals have called for the elimination or significant reduction of mandatory minimums, arguing that sentencing decisions should be based on the unique facts of each case and the principles of proportionality and individualized justice.

Another area of concern for liberals is the so-called "three-strikes" laws, which mandate life imprisonment for individuals convicted of a third serious or violent felony. These laws have been criticized for their disproportionate impact on nonviolent offenders and for exacerbating the problem of prison overcrowding. In recent years, some states have reformed their three-strikes laws to focus on truly violent offenders or to provide judges with greater discretion in sentencing. Liberals continue to push for further revisions to these laws, as well as for a broader reconsideration of the nation's approach to punishment.

Expanding the use of alternatives to incarceration is another critical component of the liberal agenda for ending mass incarceration. Programs such as drug treatment courts, mental health diversion programs, and community service options have shown promise in reducing recidivism rates and addressing the underlying causes of criminal behavior. By diverting individuals away from the traditional criminal justice system and into more rehabilitative and restorative programs, liberals argue that society can break the cycle of crime and incarceration and promote better outcomes for all involved.

In sum, the liberal push for sentencing reform and the reduction of mass incarceration is rooted in a desire to create a more just, equitable, and effective criminal justice system. By advocating for policies that emphasize rehabilitation over punishment, that take into account the individual circumstances of each case, and that prioritize community-based alternatives to imprisonment, liberals hope to transform the way America responds to crime and to foster a more compassionate and inclusive society.

7.2: Abolishing the Death Penalty and Addressing Wrongful Convictions

The death penalty remains a highly controversial and divisive issue in the United States. Liberals have long opposed capital punishment, citing concerns about its morality, effectiveness, and the risk of executing innocent people. In recent years, the movement to abolish the death penalty has gained significant momentum, with several states abolishing or placing a moratorium on executions. This section will delve into the liberal opposition to the death penalty and the ongoing efforts to end capital punishment in the United States.

One of the primary arguments against the death penalty is the moral and ethical belief that the state should not have the power to take a person's life. Many liberals argue that capital punishment is a form of cruel and unusual punishment, which is prohibited by the Eighth Amendment to the U.S. Constitution. Moreover, they contend that the death penalty does not serve as an effective deterrent to crime and that it is often applied in a racially and socioeconomically biased manner.

Another major concern for liberals is the risk of wrongful convictions and the execution of innocent people. According to the Death Penalty Information Center, more than 185 people have been exonerated from death row in the United States since 1973. These cases highlight the fallibility of the criminal justice system and the irreversible consequences of capital punishment.

To address the issue of wrongful convictions, liberals advocate for a variety of reforms aimed at enhancing the fairness and accuracy of the criminal justice process. Some of these reforms include improving eyewitness identification procedures to reduce the risk of misidentification, ensuring that all defendants have access to competent legal representation, and improving the standards and practices of forensic science to minimize the likelihood of erroneous evidence being used in court.

Liberals also emphasize the importance of providing adequate compensation and support for those who have been wrongfully convicted, as well as implementing measures to hold accountable those responsible for miscarriages of justice. This includes establishing independent commissions to investigate claims of innocence, providing avenues for post-conviction relief, and implementing policies to prevent prosecutorial misconduct.

The liberal opposition to the death penalty and commitment to addressing wrongful convictions reflect a broader commitment to justice, fairness, and human rights. By advocating for the abolition of capital punishment and pushing for reforms that enhance the accuracy and integrity of the criminal justice system, liberals seek to create a more just and humane society that values the sanctity of human life and the dignity of all individuals, regardless of their circumstances.

7.3: Community-Based Alternatives and Restorative Justice

The liberal approach to criminal justice reform also emphasizes the need for community-based alternatives to traditional punishment and the adoption of restorative justice principles. By focusing on rehabilitation, reintegration, and addressing the root causes of criminal behavior, liberals argue that these approaches can lead to more effective and humane outcomes for both offenders and their communities. This section will explore some of the key policy initiatives and restorative justice practices that have gained traction among liberals in recent years.

One of the cornerstones of community-based alternatives to punishment is the concept of problem-solving courts, such as drug treatment courts and mental health diversion programs. These specialized courts aim to address the underlying issues that contribute to criminal behavior, such as substance abuse and mental health disorders, by providing targeted interventions and support services. Rather than focusing on punishment, these courts prioritize treatment, rehabilitation, and community reintegration, with the goal of reducing recidivism and promoting long-term recovery.

Another aspect of community-based alternatives is the use of restorative justice practices, which seek to repair the harm caused by crime and promote healing for all parties involved, including victims, offenders, and the community at large. Restorative justice practices can take many forms, such as victim-offender mediation, family group conferencing, and community reparative boards. These approaches prioritize dialogue, accountability, and the active participation of all stakeholders in finding solutions that address the needs of victims, promote personal growth and transformation for offenders, and restore a sense of harmony within the community.

In addition to these specific initiatives, liberals also advocate for a broader shift in the criminal justice system's focus from punishment and retribution to prevention, rehabilitation, and social reintegration. This may include investing in community-based programs that provide education, job training, and social support for individuals at risk of involvement in criminal activity, as well as policies that reduce barriers to reentry for those with criminal records, such as expungement and the "ban the box" movement.

Overall, the liberal emphasis on community-based alternatives and restorative justice reflects a belief in the potential for redemption and personal growth, as well as a commitment to addressing the root causes of crime and promoting social cohesion. By advocating for policies and practices that prioritize rehabilitation and reintegration, liberals aim to create a more just and compassionate criminal justice system that truly serves the needs of individuals, families, and communities across the United States.

8: Immigration Reform and Inclusivity

The United States has always been a nation of immigrants, with diverse people coming together to form a rich cultural tapestry that defines the American identity. However, throughout history, immigration policies have been shaped by shifting political landscapes and varying degrees of inclusivity. In recent years, immigration reform has emerged as a prominent issue on the liberal agenda, driven by a commitment to compassion, fairness, and respect for the contributions that immigrants make to society. This chapter delves into the liberal perspective on immigration reform, discussing the key principles and policy proposals that aim to provide a pathway to citizenship for undocumented immigrants, prioritize family reunification, protect asylum seekers, and promote cultural diversity in our communities. Through a comprehensive and humane approach, liberals strive to create an inclusive and just immigration system that reflects the core values of the United States.

8.1: Pathway to Citizenship and DACA

The United States is home to approximately 11 million undocumented immigrants, many of whom have lived in the country for decades, working, paying taxes, and contributing to their communities. Despite their deep roots in American society, these individuals continue to face the constant threat of deportation, living in the shadows without access to essential rights and services. In response to this pressing issue, liberals have long advocated for comprehensive immigration reform that includes a clear and just pathway to citizenship for undocumented immigrants.

One of the central components of this push for reform is the protection and expansion of the Deferred Action for Childhood Arrivals (DACA) program. Established by the Obama administration in 2012, DACA offers temporary relief from deportation and work authorization to eligible undocumented youth who were brought to the United States as children. The program has shielded nearly 800,000 young people, known as "Dreamers," from the risk of deportation, allowing them to pursue higher education, join the workforce, and contribute to society without fear of being forcibly removed from the only country they have ever known as home.

The liberal approach to immigration reform seeks not only to preserve DACA but also to expand its reach and create a permanent solution for Dreamers, through legislation such as the DREAM Act. This proposed legislation would offer a pathway to citizenship for eligible individuals who meet certain criteria, such as completing higher education, serving in the military, or being gainfully employed. Contributing to the American dream.

In addition to advocating for Dreamers, liberals also call for a broader pathway to citizenship for the millions of other undocumented immigrants who have made the United States their home. This would involve creating a fair and accessible process for these individuals to come out of the shadows, register with the government, pay any owed taxes, and ultimately earn the right to apply for permanent residency and citizenship.

The push for a pathway to citizenship is grounded in the belief that immigrants are an essential part of the American fabric, contributing to the economy, enriching the nation's culture, and upholding its core values. By providing undocumented immigrants with a chance to fully integrate into society and access the rights and opportunities afforded to citizens, liberals argue that the United States can create a more inclusive, just, and prosperous nation for all.

8.2: Family Reunification and Asylum Seekers

One of the cornerstones of the liberal approach to immigration reform is a strong commitment to family reunification and the humane treatment of asylum seekers. This stems from the belief that families should be kept together and that people fleeing violence, persecution, or extreme hardship deserve a fair and compassionate response from the United States.

A key issue that has garnered widespread attention and concern is the practice of family separation at the border. Under the Trump administration's "zero-tolerance" policy, thousands of children were forcibly separated from their parents as they crossed the U.S.-Mexico border, leading to a humanitarian crisis and widespread condemnation from both domestic and international observers. In response, liberals have been at the forefront of efforts to end this cruel and inhumane practice, calling for the reunification of separated families and the implementation of more humane border policies.

In addition to addressing family separations, liberals also advocate for policies that support the rights of asylum seekers. These include providing legal representation for individuals navigating the complex asylum process, ensuring that they have access to accurate information and support throughout their cases. By offering legal assistance, liberals argue that asylum seekers will have a better chance of presenting their claims effectively and obtaining the protection they need.

Furthermore, the liberal agenda seeks to improve the conditions in which asylum seekers and other immigrants are held while awaiting the resolution of their cases. This involves enhancing oversight of detention facilities, ensuring that they meet basic standards of care and human rights, and promoting alternatives to detention, such as community-based programs that allow individuals to live with family members or sponsors while their cases are being processed.

By focusing on family reunification, the humane treatment of asylum seekers, and the improvement of conditions in detention facilities, liberals aim to create a more compassionate and just immigration system that aligns with the nation's core values and its long-standing tradition of offering refuge to those in need.

8.3: Cultural Diversity and Inclusive Communities

A fundamental aspect of the liberal perspective on immigration reform is the recognition and celebration of cultural diversity and the promotion of inclusive communities. Liberals believe that the United States is, at its core, a nation of immigrants, and that embracing the rich tapestry of cultural backgrounds, traditions, and experiences that immigrants bring is essential to fostering a strong, vibrant, and cohesive society.

Multiculturalism is a key tenet of the liberal outlook on immigration, emphasizing that the diverse array of cultures, languages, and beliefs that immigrants bring with them can enrich American society as a whole. The contributions of immigrants to various aspects of American life, from the economy to the arts, are immense, and liberals argue that acknowledging and appreciating this diversity is not only a moral imperative but also a practical one, as it fosters innovation, creativity, and social cohesion.

In order to promote social integration and combat xenophobia, liberals advocate for a range of initiatives and policies designed to create inclusive communities. These include education and awareness campaigns that highlight the positive contributions of immigrants and dispel myths and misconceptions about their impact on society. Such campaigns can help to counteract negative stereotypes and foster greater understanding and empathy between different cultural groups.

Liberals also support policies that prioritize language and cultural education, both for immigrants themselves and for the broader population. By providing resources and opportunities for immigrants to learn English and adapt to American customs, while also encouraging native-born Americans to learn about and appreciate the cultures of their immigrant neighbors, liberals believe that communities can become more interconnected and harmonious.

Another important aspect of the liberal approach to promoting inclusivity is the celebration of the unique heritage of immigrant communities. This involves supporting cultural events, festivals, and other initiatives that showcase the customs, arts, and traditions of different immigrant groups. By creating spaces for these communities to share and celebrate their heritage, liberals argue that the United States can foster a more inclusive and vibrant society that is enriched by the contributions of immigrants from all walks of life.

The liberal vision for immigration reform encompasses not only policies related to citizenship, family reunification, and asylum, but also a broader commitment to fostering cultural diversity and inclusive communities. Through initiatives that promote social integration, combat xenophobia, and celebrate the unique heritage of immigrant communities, liberals seek to create a more just and compassionate society that truly embodies the values of the American melting pot.

9: Gun Control and Public Safety

Gun violence has long been a pressing issue in the United States, with mass shootings, urban violence, and accidents involving firearms occurring all too frequently. The devastating impact of these incidents on families, communities, and the nation as a whole has led to a growing demand for action to curb gun violence and ensure public safety. In this chapter, we will examine the liberal perspective on gun control and the various policy proposals put forth to address this complex issue. Through a comprehensive approach that includes universal background checks, bans on assault weapons and high-capacity magazines, and community-based initiatives to prevent gun violence, liberals seek to create a safer environment for all Americans.

9.1: Universal Background Checks

Universal background checks have long been a cornerstone of the liberal approach to gun control. Advocates argue that these checks are a critical tool for preventing firearms from falling into the hands of individuals who pose a risk to themselves or others, such as criminals, domestic abusers, and those with serious mental health issues. In this section, we will explore the rationale behind universal background checks, the current gaps in the system, and the legislative efforts to tighten regulations.

The current background check system in the United States, established by the Brady Handgun Violence Prevention Act in 1993, requires federally licensed firearms dealers to perform background checks on prospective buyers through the National Instant Criminal Background Check System (NICS). While this system has successfully prevented many individuals with disqualifying criminal or mental health records from acquiring firearms, it has significant gaps that undermine its effectiveness.

Liberals have long called for the implementation of universal background checks, which would require background checks on all gun sales and transfers, including those conducted by private sellers. By regulating private sales, universal background checks would help ensure that firearms do not end up in the hands of those who pose a risk to public safety.

Several attempts have been made to pass legislation mandating universal background checks at the federal level, such as the Manchin-Toomey Amendment in 2013 and the Bipartisan Background Checks Act of 2019. Although these efforts have faced resistance from some lawmakers and interest groups, public opinion polls consistently show strong support for universal background checks among Americans across the political spectrum.

In the absence of federal action, some states have taken matters into their own hands, implementing their own universal background check laws to close the gun show loophole and regulate private sales. These state-level efforts have shown promise in reducing gun violence, providing further evidence of the potential benefits of expanding background checks nationwide.

Universal background checks are a critical component of the liberal approach to gun control, aimed at closing gaps in the current system and preventing firearms from falling into the hands of those who pose a danger to themselves or others.

9.2: Assault Weapon Bans and High-Capacity Magazine Restrictions

In recent years, the United States has seen a disturbing rise in the frequency and lethality of mass shootings. Many of these tragic events have involved the use of assault weapons and high-capacity magazines, which enable shooters to fire a large number of rounds in a short period of time, resulting in a higher number of casualties. As a result, the liberal push for gun control measures has increasingly focused on banning assault weapons and restricting high-capacity magazines in an effort to protect public safety and reduce the devastating impact of these incidents.

Assault weapons, which are typically semi-automatic firearms with military-style features, have been used in a number of high-profile mass shootings, such as the 2012 Sandy Hook Elementary School shooting, the 2016 Pulse nightclub shooting, and the 2017 Las Vegas shooting. These weapons are designed for rapid-fire and are capable of inflicting significant harm in a short period of time. Critics argue that there is no legitimate civilian use for these weapons and that their availability only serves to facilitate deadly mass shootings.

In 1994, the federal government passed the Public Safety and Recreational Firearms Use Protection Act, commonly known as the Assault Weapons Ban, which prohibited the manufacture, sale, and possession of certain semi-automatic firearms and large-capacity ammunition magazines for a period of 10 years. While the ban was in effect, research suggests that it had a positive impact on reducing gun violence. However, the ban expired in 2004 and has not been renewed, leading to renewed calls for its reinstatement.

High-capacity magazines, which allow a shooter to fire multiple rounds without needing to reload, have also been targeted by gun control advocates. By restricting the number of rounds a shooter can fire before needing to reload, high-capacity magazine restrictions have the potential to limit the lethality of mass shootings and provide opportunities for potential victims to escape or intervene. Several states have already implemented restrictions on magazine capacity, and there have been efforts at the federal level to introduce similar legislation.

Opponents of assault weapon bans and high-capacity magazine restrictions argue that these measures infringe upon Second Amendment rights and that criminals will still find ways to obtain these weapons, rendering the restrictions ineffective. However, proponents point to evidence from countries with stricter gun control measures, where mass shootings are far less common, as well as research suggesting that the 1994 Assault Weapons Ban had a positive impact on reducing gun violence during its tenure.

The liberal push for assault weapon bans and high-capacity magazine restrictions is driven by a desire to reduce the lethality of mass shootings and protect public safety. While these measures face opposition from some lawmakers and interest groups, there is a growing consensus among the public and experts alike that taking steps to limit the availability of these weapons and accessories could play a critical role in preventing future tragedies and creating a safer society for all.

What need to people have of any kind of firearm that can fire off more than ten rounds at a time? If you're hunting deer, that deer will not have any viable meat left on it and the mount will look like Swiss cheese.

9.3: Gun Violence Prevention and Community-Based Initiatives

While gun control measures such as universal background checks and assault weapon bans are essential components of the liberal approach to reducing gun violence, there is a growing recognition that a comprehensive strategy must also address the root causes of violence and involve community-based initiatives. By investing in mental health support, violence interruption programs, and social services, liberals aim to create a multi-faceted approach to gun violence prevention that goes beyond regulation and seeks to promote healthier, safer communities.

Mental health support is a crucial aspect of gun violence prevention, as mental health issues have been linked to a number of high-profile mass shootings. By increasing funding for mental health services and making them more accessible, liberals argue that society can better identify and treat individuals who may be at risk of committing acts of violence. This includes initiatives such as expanding access to counseling and therapy, implementing mental health screening programs, and providing training for educators and community members to recognize the signs of mental health crises.

Violence interruption programs have also emerged as a promising approach to reducing gun violence, particularly in urban areas. These programs, which have been implemented in cities like Chicago and New York, involve trained "violence interrupters" who work within their communities to mediate conflicts, prevent retaliation, and promote nonviolent solutions. By working closely with community members and drawing on their knowledge of local dynamics, these programs have demonstrated success in reducing gun violence and improving public safety.

Investment in social services is another key component of the liberal approach to gun violence prevention. Addressing the underlying social and economic factors that contribute to violence, such as poverty, unemployment, and lack of educational opportunities, can help create the conditions for healthier and more stable communities. Policies that prioritize investment in education, job training programs, and affordable housing can play a critical role in breaking the cycle of violence and promoting long-term safety.

In addition to these measures, liberals also advocate for robust research into the causes of gun violence and the most effective methods of prevention. By funding research and collecting data on the factors that contribute to gun violence, policymakers can make more informed decisions and develop targeted interventions to address this complex issue.

The liberal commitment to gun violence prevention goes beyond regulatory measures and seeks to address the root causes of violence through a combination of policy initiatives and community-based programs. By investing in mental health support, violence interruption initiatives, and social services, as well as supporting robust research into the issue, liberals aim to create a comprehensive approach to reducing gun violence and promoting safe, healthy communities across the United States.

10: Women's Rights and Reproductive Justice

Women's rights and reproductive justice are central to the liberal agenda, as they are deeply intertwined with gender equality, personal autonomy, and social progress. This chapter aims to provide a comprehensive understanding of the liberal commitment to promoting and protecting women's reproductive rights, while also recognizing the diverse needs and experiences of women across different racial, socioeconomic, and cultural backgrounds. By examining the importance of access to comprehensive reproductive healthcare, the ongoing struggle to safeguard abortion rights, and the broader concept of reproductive justice, we will delve into the various aspects of this critical issue and explore the policy initiatives that liberals advocate for in the pursuit of reproductive justice for all.

10.1: Access to Comprehensive Reproductive Healthcare

Access to comprehensive reproductive healthcare is a fundamental aspect of women's rights and a core component of reproductive justice. This encompasses a wide range of services, such as contraception, maternal care, family planning, and abortion care, all of which contribute to the overall health, well-being, and autonomy of women. In this section, we will explore the liberal perspective on promoting access to comprehensive reproductive healthcare, the policy initiatives aimed at ensuring affordability and availability of these services, and the importance of addressing disparities in access across different populations.

Liberals argue that access to comprehensive reproductive healthcare is a fundamental human right and a key determinant of gender equality. By empowering women to make informed decisions about their reproductive health, they can exercise greater control over their lives, pursue their aspirations, and contribute to the social and economic development of their communities. Furthermore, reproductive healthcare services such as contraception and family planning have been shown to reduce unintended pregnancies, decrease maternal and infant mortality rates, and improve the overall health outcomes for women and their families.

To promote access to comprehensive reproductive healthcare, liberals advocate for policies that address both affordability and availability of services. One such policy initiative is the funding of organizations like Planned Parenthood, which provides essential healthcare services, including contraception, cancer screenings, and sexually transmitted infection (STI) testing and treatment, to millions of women and men each year. By ensuring that these organizations receive adequate federal and state funding, liberals aim to protect access to crucial reproductive health services, particularly for low-income and uninsured individuals.

Another key policy proposal is the expansion of healthcare coverage for reproductive services. The Affordable Care Act (ACA) made significant strides in this area by requiring most insurance plans to cover contraceptive methods and services without cost-sharing. However, some conservatives have sought to undermine this provision, arguing that it infringes on religious freedom. Liberals maintain that the benefits of expanded coverage, including improved health outcomes and reduced healthcare costs, far outweigh any potential infringement on religious liberty, and they continue to push for policies that protect and expand access to contraceptive coverage.

Despite these efforts, disparities in access to reproductive healthcare persist, particularly for women of color, low-income women, and those living in rural areas. To address these disparities, liberals advocate for targeted investments in community-based organizations, the expansion of telehealth services, and initiatives aimed at addressing the social determinants of health that contribute to these disparities. By focusing on these policy interventions, the liberal agenda seeks to ensure that all women, regardless of their background or location, have access to the comprehensive reproductive healthcare they need and deserve.

10.2: Protecting Abortion Rights and Roe v. Wade

The liberal commitment to protecting abortion rights and preserving the landmark Supreme Court decision in Roe v. Wade has long been a critical aspect of the broader fight for women's rights and reproductive justice. However, with the recent overturning of Roe v. Wade by a conservative Supreme Court, the battle for abortion rights has taken on a new urgency. This section will examine the ongoing legal and political struggles over abortion access, the role of the judiciary in shaping reproductive rights, and the importance of appointing judges who respect reproductive rights and the constitutional right to privacy.

The 1973 Supreme Court decision in Roe v. Wade established the constitutional right to abortion, rooted in the right to privacy protected by the Fourteenth Amendment's Due Process Clause. For decades, this landmark ruling has served as the cornerstone of reproductive rights in the United States, ensuring that women have the ability to make their own decisions about their pregnancies. However, since its inception, Roe v. Wade has faced significant opposition from conservative lawmakers, activists, and judges who seek to restrict or eliminate access to abortion services.

With the recent overturning of Roe v. Wade, the landscape of abortion rights in the United States has changed dramatically. States are now free to regulate or even ban abortion entirely, leading to a patchwork of laws that vary widely from one state to another. This has resulted in significant barriers to access for many women, particularly those in states with strict anti-abortion legislation. These restrictions disproportionately impact low-income women and women of color, who may lack the resources to travel to states with more lenient abortion laws.

In light of these developments, the liberal response has been to redouble efforts to protect abortion rights at the state and federal levels. This includes advocating for legislation that enshrines the right to abortion in state constitutions, as well as pushing for federal laws that guarantee access to abortion services nationwide. These efforts also involve supporting candidates who are committed to defending reproductive rights and who will appoint judges who respect the constitutional right to privacy.

The appointment of judges who respect reproductive rights is particularly crucial in the ongoing struggle over abortion access. The judiciary plays a key role in interpreting and shaping reproductive rights, and the recent overturning of Roe v. Wade has demonstrated the profound impact that a conservative Supreme Court can have on this issue. By supporting judicial nominees who are committed to upholding reproductive rights and the constitutional right to privacy, liberals aim to ensure that future legal battles over abortion access are decided in a manner that protects and preserves the right to choose.

The liberal commitment to protecting abortion rights and preserving the legacy of Roe v. Wade remains steadfast, even in the face of significant legal and political challenges. By advocating for legislation that safeguards access to abortion services, supporting candidates who champion reproductive rights, and promoting the appointment of judges who respect the constitutional right to privacy, liberals continue to fight for the fundamental principle that every woman should have the right to make her own decisions about her body and her reproductive health.

10.3: Reproductive Justice and Intersectionality

The pursuit of reproductive justice extends beyond the specific issue of abortion rights and includes a broader spectrum of concerns that affect women's reproductive lives. This holistic approach acknowledges the complex intersection of various social, economic, and political factors that influence women's health outcomes. An intersectional perspective recognizes the multiple, interlocking forms of discrimination and disadvantage that women, especially women of color, low-income women, and LGBTQ+ individuals, may experience. In this section, we will delve into the concept of reproductive justice, discuss its roots and significance, and examine the importance of addressing these intersectional disparities in the fight for women's rights.

The term "reproductive justice" was coined by a collective of African American women in 1994 and is rooted in a human rights framework. Reproductive justice advocates argue that the ability of any woman to determine her own reproductive destiny is directly linked to the conditions in her community—and these conditions are shaped by both social and economic policies. Therefore, reproductive justice is not just about the right not to have a child, but also the right to have children and to parent them in safe and healthy environments.

Reproductive justice goes beyond the scope of reproductive health and rights to encompass issues of environmental justice, immigration rights, economic inequality, education, and more. It recognizes that these issues are not separate from one another but are deeply interconnected. For instance, a low-income woman living in a polluted neighborhood may not only have difficulty accessing healthcare services but also face an increased risk of adverse health outcomes due to environmental hazards. Similarly, immigration status can affect a woman's ability to access reproductive healthcare and other social services.

Intersectionality, a term coined by legal scholar Kimberlé Crenshaw, is a framework for understanding how aspects of a person's social and political identities might combine to create unique modes of discrimination and privilege.

Intersectionality within the context of reproductive justice recognizes that women do not live single-issue lives and that efforts to achieve reproductive justice must take into account the multiple identities and experiences of women. It demands that we understand and address the unique challenges faced by women of color, LGBTQ+ individuals, and low-income women when it comes to reproductive healthcare and rights.

For example, women of color face substantial disparities in reproductive health outcomes, including higher rates of maternal mortality and morbidity. These disparities are the result of systemic racism, which manifests in the healthcare system through implicit bias, lower quality care, and lack of access to services.

Similarly, LGBTQ+ individuals often face barriers to reproductive healthcare, including discrimination, lack of provider knowledge and understanding, and exclusion from health insurance coverage. For low-income women, the ability to access reproductive healthcare services is often hindered by economic barriers, including the high cost of healthcare and lack of insurance.

Liberals argue that achieving reproductive justice requires addressing these intersectional disparities through comprehensive, culturally competent policies and practices. This includes efforts to eliminate racial and socioeconomic disparities in reproductive health outcomes, ensure healthcare access for all women regardless of income, race, or immigration status, and promote LGBTQ+ inclusive reproductive healthcare.

The concept of reproductive justice offers a broader and more nuanced perspective on women's rights, one that acknowledges the multifaceted nature of women's experiences and the intersectional disparities that exist in reproductive health outcomes. By adopting an intersectional approach to women's rights and reproductive justice, liberals aim to address the systemic inequalities that affect women's reproductive lives and to ensure that all women have the ability to make decisions about their bodies and their reproductive health.

11: Voting Rights and Democracy

The right to vote is at the heart of any democracy. It is the fundamental mechanism by which citizens shape the laws that govern them and the leaders who implement them. It is through this critical act that individuals can have a direct influence on the social and political landscapes that directly impact their lives. Unfortunately, in many areas across the United States, this foundational right is being challenged, restricted, or outright denied, making it a central issue for liberals and progressives alike.

The fundamental belief that underpins this discussion is that every citizen, regardless of their race, socio-economic status, or previous criminal convictions, should have an equal and unhindered right to vote. Liberal proponents argue that our democratic system can only function effectively when it is representative of the people it serves, and this can only be achieved through the active protection and promotion of universal suffrage. As we journey through this chapter, we will uncover the strategies and policies liberals advocate for to uphold this vision of an inclusive and representative democracy.

11.1: Universal Suffrage and Voting Accessibility

The pursuit of universal suffrage - the right to vote for every citizen - is a foundational aspect of liberal policy. Liberals believe that democracy can only thrive when every citizen, regardless of their socio-economic status, race, or past criminal convictions, can exercise their right to vote freely and conveniently. There are several key strategies and policies that liberals advocate for to achieve this, including automatic voter registration, the expansion of early voting and vote-by-mail options, and the restoration of voting rights for former felons.

Automatic voter registration is a policy that would automatically enroll eligible citizens to vote when they interact with government agencies, unless they opt out. This could include when they register a vehicle, apply for a driver's license, or apply for social services. Liberals argue that automatic voter registration could significantly increase voter turnout by making registration easier and more convenient, particularly for young people, low-income individuals, and people of color who may be less likely to be registered to vote.

Alongside automatic voter registration, liberals push for the expansion of early voting and vote-by-mail options. They argue that voting on a single day, traditionally a working day, may not be convenient or even possible for many individuals due to work, family commitments, or other obstacles. By offering a broader range of voting options, liberals believe that we can enable more citizens to cast their votes and participate in the democratic process.

The issue of felon disenfranchisement, the loss of voting rights due to criminal conviction, is another area where liberals advocate for change. In many states, individuals with felony convictions lose their right to vote, sometimes permanently. This has led to a large number of Americans being excluded from the democratic process. Liberals argue for policies that restore voting rights to former felons who have completed their sentences, believing that they should have the opportunity to re-engage with society and participate in the democratic process.

Liberals view voting not only as a right but as a cornerstone of an active and representative democracy. By advocating for policies like automatic voter registration, expanded early voting and vote-by-mail options, and the restoration of voting rights for former felons, liberals aim to create a more inclusive and accessible democratic process. They believe that these measures can help to ensure that our democracy truly represents and serves all citizens, not just a privileged few.

11.2: Combatting Voter Suppression and Disenfranchisement

Voter suppression and disenfranchisement represent significant threats to a thriving democracy. These tactics, which disproportionately impact marginalized communities, are seen by liberals as severe obstacles to achieving a representative democracy. In response, liberals have developed numerous policy proposals to combat these challenges and ensure the voting rights of all citizens.

The tools of voter suppression are many and varied. They can include onerous voter ID laws, the purging of voter rolls, restriction of early voting and absentee voting, closure or relocation of polling places, and more. While these measures are often justified under the guise of maintaining the integrity of elections, liberals argue that they disproportionately impact marginalized groups—people of color, low-income individuals, and young voters—effectively making it harder for them to vote.

To counteract these suppression efforts, liberals champion policies that make voting easier and more accessible. These policies can include the relaxation of strict voter ID laws, prevention of unfair purges of voter rolls, and extension of early voting periods. They also advocate for clear and consistent information about voting procedures and locations of polling places to avoid confusion or misinformation.

Furthermore, liberals have long been vocal about the need for legislation to restore the protections of the Voting Rights Act, which was weakened by the Supreme Court decision in Shelby County v. Holder in 2013. This decision removed federal oversight of voting laws in states with histories of discriminatory practices, leading to an uptick in voter suppression laws. Liberals argue that restoring and even expanding the Voting Rights Act is essential to protect the voting rights of marginalized communities.

Disenfranchisement also extends to gerrymandering—the manipulation of electoral boundaries to favor one party. Liberals seek to reform the redistricting process by advocating for independent commissions, which can create more balanced electoral districts and ensure fair representation.

In the eyes of liberals, the struggle against voter suppression and disenfranchisement is a struggle for democracy itself. By advocating for more accessible voting procedures, stronger protections against discriminatory practices, and fairer electoral districts, liberals aim to create a political system in which every citizen can participate fully and equally.

11.3: Ending Gerrymandering and Promoting Fair Representation

One of the most insidious challenges to democratic representation is the issue of gerrymandering, the practice of manipulating electoral boundaries to favor a particular political party. This practice often results in 'safe seats', where incumbents face little to no competition, thereby reducing the power of voters' voices. For liberals, gerrymandering is a grave concern that undermines the principle of equal representation. As such, the call for redistricting reform lies at the core of the liberal agenda for voting rights and democracy.

To combat gerrymandering, liberals propose a series of measures aimed at making the redistricting process more fair and transparent. Among these initiatives is the establishment of independent redistricting commissions, entities separate from the partisan influences of state legislatures. These commissions would be responsible for drawing district lines in a way that reflects the demographic diversity of the state and ensures fair competition among candidates. Models for such commissions already exist in states like California and Arizona, where redistricting is performed by citizen-led commissions with members from different political affiliations.

Alongside independent redistricting commissions, liberals also advocate for the use of algorithmic models in the district drawing process. These models can generate maps based on nonpartisan criteria, such as population equality, contiguity, and respect for community boundaries. By eliminating the influence of partisan gerrymandering, these algorithms can help create electoral maps that more accurately reflect the political landscape of a given region.

However, redistricting reform is not without its challenges. Legal battles, logistical hurdles, and entrenched partisan interests can all stand in the way of change. Nevertheless, liberals argue that the fight against gerrymandering is a crucial step towards a more representative democracy. By pushing for independent redistricting commissions and the use of fair mapping algorithms, liberals hope to ensure that every vote counts and every voice is heard. Their goal is a political system that truly embodies the democratic principle: one person, one vote.

We recognize the centrality of voting rights and the health of our democracy to the liberal agenda. The expansion of universal suffrage, the safeguarding against voter suppression, and the commitment to combat gerrymandering, all serve the purpose of amplifying every citizen's voice, and creating a society that respects and cherishes the equality of each vote.

Each policy proposal and initiative outlined in this chapter, whether it be automatic voter registration, improved voting accessibility, or ending gerrymandering, is guided by the core liberal belief in an inclusive, fair, and representative democracy. These commitments not only reflect a deep-seated value for democratic principles but also an unyielding optimism that a more just and equitable democratic system can be realized.

As we move forward in the 21st century, the need to protect and expand voting rights and strengthen our democratic systems becomes increasingly important. In an era of increasing partisanship and social change, it is crucial that the pillars of our democracy adapt and evolve to meet the challenges of our time. This liberal commitment to the integrity of our democratic systems is not just about winning elections, it's about preserving the fundamental principles that make the United States a beacon of democratic governance.

The task of strengthening and safeguarding our democracy is a collective one, requiring the active participation of citizens, the courage of our lawmakers, and the vigilance of institutions. It's a challenge that spans beyond party lines, reaching into the heart of what it means to be an American. In the face of these challenges, the liberal vision remains steadfast and clear: a more inclusive, fair, and representative democracy where every voice matters, and every vote counts.

12: Labor Rights and Workers' Protections

From the early days of the labor movement, marked by the struggle for fair wages and humane working conditions, to today's fight for wage equity and the right to organize, the quest for labor rights has been a defining aspect of our nation's history. At its core, it is a testament to the enduring power of the American worker in shaping not just our economy, but the very fabric of our society.

The liberal perspective has long upheld the rights of workers as a critical element of a just society. It embraces the belief that every individual who contributes their labor to the prosperity of the nation deserves respect, dignity, and a fair share of the wealth they help generate. It contends that labor is not merely a commodity, but an expression of human effort, deserving of fair remuneration, safe working conditions, and legal protection from exploitation.

12.1: Collective Bargaining and Union Support

At the heart of the liberal philosophy on labor rights is the principle of collective bargaining and strong union support. Collective bargaining—the process by which working people, through their unions, negotiate contracts with their employers to determine their terms of employment—represents the embodiment of workplace democracy. This essential democratic process affirms the notion that labor is not a mere commodity but an indispensable element of the productive capacity of any society.

Unions have a storied history of securing transformative changes in the workplace, including the 40-hour workweek, minimum wage laws, healthcare benefits, and safer working conditions. They serve as a countervailing power against the potential excesses of corporate interests, balancing the scales and giving workers a voice in their working conditions and compensation.

Liberals have consistently championed the rights of unions, recognizing them as indispensable for fostering a fair and thriving workforce. They have backed policy proposals designed to protect and strengthen unions, such as the Protecting the Right to Organize (PRO) Act. This legislation seeks to prevent the misclassification of employees as independent contractors, impose stricter penalties on employers who retaliate against union organizing, and safeguard the right to strike.

Moreover, liberals advocate for sectoral bargaining, a practice where unions negotiate for workers across an entire industry, not just at individual workplaces. This form of collective bargaining has the potential to create industry-wide standards, lifting wages and improving conditions for all workers in the sector, including those not in a union.

Support for collective bargaining extends to public sector employees, including teachers, firefighters, and public health workers. Liberals have fought against measures that aim to strip these workers of their rights to unionize and collectively negotiate their terms of employment.

The liberal commitment to collective bargaining and union support reflects a deep-seated belief in the power of collective action and solidarity among workers. It champions the idea that when workers unite to negotiate their terms of employment, they are not just bargaining for better wages or benefits but are also advocating for dignity, respect, and fairness in the workplace.

12.2: Workplace Safety and Regulatory Oversight

Workplace safety is a paramount concern in the liberal agenda for labor rights. With roots dating back to the Progressive Era's labor movements and the establishment of the Occupational Safety and Health Administration (OSHA) in 1970, the advocacy for workers' safety and health has been a cornerstone of the liberal approach to labor rights.

Liberals firmly believe that no worker should risk their life or health to make a living. This view acknowledges the inherent dignity of every worker and the principle that the human value of a worker transcends their economic productivity. To this end, strict workplace safety regulations and effective regulatory oversight are viewed as vital tools to ensure workers are not exposed to unnecessary risks.

OSHA, the federal agency tasked with ensuring safe and healthy working conditions, plays a critical role in the liberal vision for labor rights. The agency sets and enforces protective workplace safety and health standards, provides training, outreach, education, and assistance to ensure these standards are met. However, liberals argue that in recent years, OSHA has been chronically underfunded and understaffed, limiting its capacity to conduct inspections and enforce its standards effectively.

The liberal perspective advocates for strengthening OSHA and other similar regulatory bodies by increasing their funding, enhancing their enforcement powers, and expanding their reach. The aim is to have a robust and proactive regulatory system that not only responds to workplace accidents but anticipates and prevents them.

Furthermore, liberals back policies that require employers to provide comprehensive health and safety training to their workers, report all workplace injuries and illnesses, and protect whistleblowers who report safety violations. There is also a growing call within liberal circles to extend OSHA's jurisdiction to cover workers currently left out, including public sector workers in many states and those classified as independent contractors.

Finally, in an era of rapid technological advances and changing work environments, liberals stress the need for continuous review and updating of safety standards. This includes addressing new and emerging risks like those associated with automation, precarious gig economy jobs, and the mental health impact of work.

Workplace safety and regulatory oversight are central to the liberal view on labor rights. It is about protecting workers from preventable harm, empowering them with the knowledge and tools to protect themselves, and holding employers accountable for providing safe and healthy work environments.

12.3: Fair Labor Practices and Wage Equity

At the core of the liberal agenda for labor rights is a commitment to fair labor practices and wage equity. This commitment is grounded in the belief that all workers, irrespective of their job, deserve to be compensated fairly for their labor, to work under conditions that respect their dignity and rights, and to have a voice in the workplace.

Minimum wage laws play a central role in these efforts. For liberals, ensuring a robust minimum wage that keeps pace with inflation and cost of living increases is an essential policy tool for lifting workers out of poverty, reducing income inequality, and promoting economic justice. They argue that the current federal minimum wage is far from a living wage and advocate for its increase. Some liberals go further, arguing for a $15 per hour minimum wage or tying the minimum wage to the median wage to ensure that all workers share in economic growth.

In addition to advocating for a higher minimum wage, liberals also aim to combat wage theft, a widespread and often overlooked issue where employers violate labor laws by not paying workers the full wages to which they are legally entitled. This can take various forms, such as forcing employees to work off the clock, failing to pay overtime wages, or simply not paying workers at all. Liberals argue for stronger enforcement of wage and hour laws, stricter penalties for violations, and better protections for workers who report wage theft.

Wage equity between different groups is another key concern. Despite significant progress, persistent wage gaps remain between men and women, between white workers and workers of color, and between workers with and without disabilities. Liberals push for policies to address these disparities, such as stronger equal pay laws, paid family and medical leave, affordable child care, and measures to combat employment discrimination.

The drive for wage equity also extends to ensuring fair compensation for overtime. Liberals largely support measures like the Obama-era overtime rule, which would have expanded the number of workers eligible for overtime pay. They argue that such measures are necessary to prevent employers from exploiting salaried workers by requiring excessive hours without additional compensation.

The liberal commitment to fair labor practices and wage equity reflects a broader vision of economic justice, where the fruits of economic growth are shared more evenly, and all workers are valued and treated with dignity. This vision recognizes that the strength and prosperity of a society depend not only on the wealth it generates but also on how that wealth is distributed.

As this chapter on labor rights and worker protections comes to a close, we must take a moment to look towards the future, recognizing both the strides made and the challenges that still lie ahead.

For liberals, the path forward is rooted in deepening the protections for workers and advancing labor rights in all sectors of the economy. This means pushing for policies that bolster collective bargaining, amplify the voice of workers, and ensure fair labor practices across the board. It also involves steadfast commitment to ensuring safe and dignified working conditions, free from hazards and exploitative practices.

In the future, we will also have to grapple with new challenges presented by the changing nature of work. The rise of the gig economy, for instance, poses questions about how labor rights and protections can be extended to non-traditional work arrangements.

How we define employees and employers, and how we ensure rights and protections for freelancers, gig workers, and other independent contractors will become increasingly critical issues.

Similarly, the ongoing automation of work will require a reimagining of labor rights and worker protections. As robots and algorithms increasingly perform tasks once done by humans, we will need to consider how to protect workers' rights and well-being in an economy where the nature of work is fundamentally shifting.

We should also remain cognizant of the disparities in labor rights and protections that exist among different groups of workers, particularly marginalized communities. Addressing these disparities will necessitate a continued commitment to intersectionality and social justice in our labor policies and practices.

As we face these challenges, it is the steadfast belief of liberals that labor rights are human rights. Safeguarding these rights is both a moral imperative and a crucial aspect of building a just and equitable society. While the work of advancing labor rights and worker protections is ongoing, the liberal agenda remains committed to standing with workers and advocating for their rights. In the end, the vision is clear: a future where all workers enjoy the protections they deserve, where their voices are heard, and where their labor is justly rewarded. With this vision as our guiding light, the fight for labor rights and worker protections carries on.

13: LGBTQ+ Rights and Equality

The fabric of any society is enriched by the diverse threads that weave it together, and the fight for equality for all members of society is central to the liberal ethos. An integral part of this struggle is the fight for the rights and equality of lesbian, gay, bisexual, transgender, and queer (LGBTQ+) individuals.

The past few decades have seen significant strides in the fight for LGBTQ+ rights, marking a clear shift from a time when being open about one's sexual orientation or gender identity could result in societal ostracism, legal penalties, or even death. Today, we celebrate an era where the rights to love and live openly are increasingly recognized and protected.

However, despite the progress that has been made, the journey is far from over. The rights and freedoms of LGBTQ+ individuals continue to face opposition and challenges across many fronts. LGBTQ+ individuals still encounter prejudice and discrimination in numerous aspects of their lives, including their workplaces, their communities, and even within their families. Transgender and non-binary individuals, in particular, face unique hurdles, battling not just for acceptance, but for recognition and respect of their very identities.

13.1: Marriage Equality and Family Rights

The fight for marriage equality has been a defining chapter in the broader struggle for LGBTQ+ rights. The legalization of same-sex marriage in the United States in 2015, following the landmark Supreme Court ruling in Obergefell v. Hodges, marked a significant victory for the LGBTQ+ community. This decision affirmed that love knows no boundaries, and the legal recognition of same-sex marriages affirmed the equal dignity and worth of all individuals, regardless of their sexual orientation.

Liberals have been at the forefront of this battle, advocating for marriage equality as a fundamental human right. This commitment is rooted in the belief that everyone deserves to form a legally recognized family unit, reaping the societal benefits and protections that come with it. It is a commitment grounded in the ideals of love, acceptance, and equality for all.

Yet, despite the legal recognition of same-sex marriages, LGBTQ+ families continue to face challenges. Adoption rights, for example, remain a contentious issue. While federal law does not prohibit LGBTQ+ individuals and couples from adopting, state laws vary significantly. Some states have even sought to enact laws that allow adoption agencies to refuse services to same-sex couples based on religious beliefs. These laws not only discriminate against LGBTQ+ individuals and couples, but they also deprive countless children of the chance to find loving, nurturing homes.

Liberals advocate for clear, unequivocal federal protections that ensure all LGBTQ+ individuals and couples have the same adoption rights as their heterosexual counterparts. The belief is that adoption decisions should be guided by the best interests of the child, and no capable, loving potential parent should be excluded based on their sexual orientation or gender identity.

Moreover, rights related to assisted reproductive technology, surrogacy, and parental recognition also require attention. Many LGBTQ+ couples rely on these methods to start their families, yet they often face complex legal hurdles. Liberals are dedicated to ensuring that these rights are guaranteed and protected, allowing all families to thrive, regardless of how they are formed.

In advocating for these rights, the liberal perspective underscores the need to view LGBTQ+ rights as human rights. Marriage equality, adoption rights, and family rights are not special privileges, but rather fundamental rights that should be afforded to all, regardless of who they love or how they identify. The struggle for these rights is part of a larger fight for equality and acceptance, a fight that continues to be a cornerstone of the liberal agenda.

13.2: Legal Protections and Anti-Discrimination Laws

Equal rights and protections under the law form the bedrock of any democratic society. For the LGBTQ+ community, however, these protections have not always been guaranteed or consistently applied. Despite the significant strides made in recent decades, discrimination based on sexual orientation and gender identity remains a pervasive issue, affecting multiple areas of life, including employment, housing, and access to public services. This is a reality that liberals are fervently committed to changing.

In the realm of employment, discrimination can manifest in numerous ways, from hiring bias to wage inequality and wrongful termination. Until recently, federal law did not expressly protect employees from discrimination on the basis of sexual orientation or gender identity. The Supreme Court's 2020 ruling in Bostock v. Clayton County, however, marked a significant turning point. The court held that Title VII of the Civil Rights Act of 1964, which prohibits employment discrimination on the basis of sex, also encompasses sexual orientation and gender identity. This landmark ruling was a major victory, yet more work remains to ensure that these protections are robustly enforced and that all LGBTQ+ individuals can work in environments free from discrimination and prejudice.

On the housing front, LGBTQ+ individuals are disproportionately affected by homelessness and housing insecurity. Discrimination plays a significant role in these challenges, with numerous reports of LGBTQ+ individuals and families being denied housing or evicted based on their sexual orientation or gender identity. To combat this, liberals advocate for strengthening and enforcing the Fair Housing Act, to explicitly outlaw housing discrimination on the basis of sexual orientation and gender identity.

Access to public services is another critical area requiring strong anti-discrimination protections. This includes access to healthcare, education, and other essential services. For example, ensuring that transgender individuals can access gender-affirming healthcare without discrimination is a crucial aspect of LGBTQ+ rights. In the educational context, combating discrimination and bullying against LGBTQ+ students is of paramount importance.

Liberals champion the passage and enforcement of comprehensive federal legislation, such as the proposed Equality Act, which would provide clear, consistent protections for LGBTQ+ individuals in these and other key areas of life. This legislation would amend existing civil rights laws, including the Civil Rights Act of 1964, to explicitly include sexual orientation and gender identity as protected characteristics.

In advocating for these measures, liberals underscore the belief that no one should face discrimination because of who they are or whom they love. Legal protections and anti-discrimination laws are not only about prohibiting harmful actions; they are about affirming the value and dignity of all individuals and ensuring that everyone has an equal opportunity to thrive.

13.3: Social Acceptance and Transgender Rights

The battle for LGBTQ+ rights is as much a fight for social acceptance and understanding as it is a legal and political struggle. It is about dismantling deeply ingrained prejudices and promoting a society that is inclusive, compassionate, and respectful of everyone's rights to self-expression and self-determination. This fight is particularly pertinent for transgender and non-binary individuals, who often face unique challenges and heightened discrimination.

Transgender and non-binary individuals experience various forms of marginalization, from social ostracization to legislative attempts to curtail their rights. The liberal agenda advocates for their full inclusion in society and respect for their identities. This includes promoting understanding and acceptance of the concept of gender identity, which extends beyond the binary notion of male and female to encompass a spectrum of identities that may not align with the sex assigned at birth.

One of the primary policy areas of focus is the right of transgender and non-binary individuals to have their gender identity recognized on legal documents, such as driver's licenses and passports. This recognition is crucial for their ability to navigate life in ways that most people take for granted, from applying for jobs to traveling. Liberals also advocate for laws protecting transgender individuals from discrimination in areas such as employment, housing, and healthcare, recognizing that transgender individuals often face heightened obstacles in these areas.

Another critical aspect of transgender rights is healthcare access. Transgender individuals often encounter barriers to obtaining necessary medical care, including gender-affirming treatments such as hormone replacement therapy and surgeries. Here, the liberal perspective emphasizes the need to eliminate these barriers and ensure that healthcare providers are educated and respectful of transgender health needs. This extends to mental health support, given the increased rates of mental health issues, including anxiety and depression, among transgender individuals due to societal stigma and discrimination.

The issue of transgender rights also intersects significantly with youth rights. Transgender and non-binary youth often face substantial difficulties, from bullying in schools to legislative efforts that aim to limit their participation in sports or access to gender-affirming healthcare. Addressing these issues is a priority in the liberal agenda, emphasizing the importance of supportive families, schools, and communities in fostering the well-being and development of transgender and non-binary youth.

The advancement of transgender rights and broader social acceptance is viewed not only as a matter of justice for transgender individuals but also as part of the larger fight for human rights and dignity. By advocating for the rights and inclusion of transgender and non-binary individuals, liberals are pushing for a society where everyone is recognized and valued for who they are, irrespective of their gender identity.

As we close this chapter on LGBTQ+ Rights and Equality, it's important to reflect on the journey we have taken and to look ahead to the road that remains. From the fight for marriage equality to the struggle for transgender rights, the past several decades have seen considerable strides towards LGBTQ+ inclusivity. Yet, much work still remains to be done.

Looking forward, the focus of the liberal agenda will continue to evolve as our understanding of gender and sexuality broadens and deepens. The fight for LGBTQ+ rights is not confined to legal battles alone, but extends to societal attitudes, cultural norms, and the preservation of human dignity. Liberals will continue to push for laws and policies that reflect these evolving understandings and that protect all people from discrimination, regardless of their sexual orientation or gender identity.

At the heart of this endeavor is the notion of intersectionality – the recognition that individuals' identities overlap in ways that can compound discrimination and marginalization. The liberal agenda for LGBTQ+ rights, therefore, will remain firmly rooted in this intersectional understanding, recognizing the need to address the unique challenges faced by individuals who belong to multiple marginalized groups.

Transgender rights, particularly the rights of transgender youth, will continue to be a key area of focus in the years to come. The aim will not only be about securing legal protections but also about fostering a culture of acceptance, where all individuals feel safe and affirmed in their identities. This is about more than policy – it's about compassion, understanding, and respect for all people in their full humanity.

The fight for LGBTQ+ rights is also, ultimately, a fight for the soul of our democracy – a fight to ensure that all people are treated with dignity and respect and that our society lives up to its promise of equality and justice for all. It's about making sure that every individual – no matter who they are or whom they love – has the freedom to live authentically and the opportunity to pursue happiness. In the future that liberals envision, no one will be left behind.

The journey towards LGBTQ+ equality is emblematic of the broader liberal endeavor: the quest for a society where every individual is recognized, valued, and treated with dignity. As we turn the page to the next chapter, we are reminded of our shared humanity, our shared struggle, and our shared commitment to making the world a better place. And so, the struggle continues, always with an eye towards a future that is more inclusive, more compassionate, and more just.

14: Racial Justice and Systemic Racism

As we turn the pages of history, we come face-to-face with a stark reality — the deeply entrenched roots of systemic racism in America. These roots have permeated our institutions, policies, and practices, persisting till this day and shaping experiences of racial and ethnic minorities. The fight against this invisible, yet incredibly potent, adversary is complex and daunting. However, it is a fight that must be fought, and a cause that must be championed, as we aspire to form a more perfect, equitable, and just union.

Recognizing systemic racism is not about apportioning blame, but rather understanding our shared history and acknowledging the latent biases within our societal structures. It is about examining the lasting effects of past injustices and working towards correcting these entrenched disparities.

The liberal agenda seeks to address systemic racism in a holistic manner, targeting the racial disparities in housing, education, and economic opportunities. The pursuit of this agenda is not just a matter of moral and social justice, but an essential pathway to achieving our nation's full potential.

As we delve into the policies and initiatives aimed at confronting systemic racism and promoting racial justice, we shall also shed light on the continuous fight to dismantle this deep-seated prejudice. The fight for racial justice is a long one, but the hope is that with understanding, effort, and commitment, we can collectively shape a future where equity and justice are not just ideals, but lived realities for all.

14.1: Understanding Systemic Racism and Its Impacts

Understanding systemic racism is the first step in addressing it. The liberal perspective holds that systemic racism, also known as institutional or structural racism, is not merely a matter of personal bias or prejudice but is embedded within our societal systems and institutions. It is perpetuated through policies, laws, and societal norms that may appear race-neutral on the surface but disproportionately impact racial and ethnic minorities in practice.

Systemic racism finds its origins in the historical context of the United States. Beginning with the institution of slavery, followed by the era of Jim Crow, segregation, redlining, and other discriminatory practices, systemic racism has a long, intricate, and painful history. These practices may have been legally abolished, but their effects are far from eradicated. They've created a ripple effect that is felt across generations, manifesting in disparities in wealth, education, housing, and criminal justice, among others.

Economic inequality is a glaring example of systemic racism's impact. The racial wealth gap, driven by discriminatory practices like redlining and wage disparities, has persisted and even widened over time. Data shows that the average wealth of white families is significantly higher than that of Black families — a discrepancy that cannot be attributed solely to individual actions but is a consequence of systemic forces.

Similarly, the American education system exhibits racial disparities, where minority-majority schools are frequently underfunded, leading to an achievement gap. This educational disparity has far-reaching impacts, affecting future employment, income levels, and social mobility.

In the criminal justice system, systemic racism manifests in the form of racial profiling, harsher sentencing, and over-policing in minority communities. Disproportionate rates of incarceration among people of color have long-term effects, not just on the individuals involved, but also on their families and communities.

The liberal understanding of systemic racism demands a comprehensive and multi-dimensional approach to address these disparities. It calls for examining and reforming the underlying structures, policies, and biases that perpetuate racial inequalities. It argues for the importance of not just legal but also social, economic, and political changes to dismantle systemic racism and create a more equitable society. Acknowledging systemic racism and understanding its far-reaching impacts is a crucial part of this process. Only then can we begin to imagine and work towards transformative change.

14.2: Addressing Racial Disparities in Housing, Education, and Economy

The liberal perspective advocates for robust and decisive action to tackle racial disparities, recognizing that systemic racism permeates various aspects of life including housing, education, and the economy. Addressing these disparities requires more than recognizing the problem – it demands targeted policies that aim to dismantle the entrenched structures perpetuating these inequalities.

In the area of housing, liberals champion laws and policies designed to counteract the impacts of decades of discriminatory practices like redlining and housing discrimination. This includes enforcing and strengthening the Fair Housing Act, which prohibits discrimination in the sale, rental, and financing of housing. Moreover, there is a push to invest in affordable housing programs and provide housing assistance to those in need. They also advocate for mortgage lending reforms to ensure equal access to home loans, acknowledging the critical role of homeownership in building generational wealth.

Regarding education, liberals are cognizant of the stark racial disparities that exist. Majority-minority schools often face chronic underfunding, leading to fewer resources and poorer outcomes for students. In response, liberals propose measures such as increased federal funding for public schools, with additional supports directed toward schools in low-income areas. They also advocate for policies to ensure diversity in schools and counteract the effects of racial segregation. Furthermore, initiatives to expand access to early childhood education programs, which have been shown to significantly improve future educational outcomes, are often emphasized.

When it comes to the economy, addressing racial disparities involves tackling wage gaps and unequal access to job opportunities. Liberals endorse raising the federal minimum wage as a step toward economic justice, given that people of color are overrepresented in low-wage jobs. They also support strengthening labor protections to counteract exploitation and promoting diversity in the workplace. Additionally, liberals call for rigorous enforcement of anti-discrimination laws in employment.

Another major economic issue is the racial wealth gap. To address this, liberals suggest a combination of wealth-building strategies such as promoting access to affordable financial services, supporting minority-owned businesses, and exploring proposals like baby bonds, a program that would provide every child with a government-funded savings account.

Overall, the liberal agenda for addressing racial disparities in housing, education, and the economy is multifaceted and interconnected, reflecting the complex nature of systemic racism. It underscores the importance of not only promoting racial diversity but also ensuring racial equity – a condition where one's racial identity is not an obstacle to access opportunities. Ultimately, the goal is to create a society where everyone has the resources and opportunities they need to thrive, regardless of their racial or ethnic background.

14.3: Policy Initiatives for Racial Justice and Equity

Committed to dismantling systemic racism and advancing racial justice, liberals champion policy initiatives that address these issues at every level of society, from criminal justice reform to healthcare accessibility.

In the realm of criminal justice, the liberal stance advocates for an end to practices that disproportionately impact people of color. This includes the over-policing of Black and Brown communities, discriminatory sentencing practices, and racial profiling. As previously discussed in previous chapters, liberals endorse various strategies such as ending cash bail, abolishing private prisons, and implementing community policing initiatives. The ultimate goal is to create a justice system that is fair, equitable, and focused on rehabilitation rather than punishment.

In healthcare, liberals acknowledge the stark racial disparities present, with people of color often experiencing lower-quality care, fewer medical resources, and higher rates of health issues like heart disease, diabetes, and COVID-19. The liberal perspective calls for policies that ensure equal access to quality healthcare for all individuals, regardless of race or ethnicity. This includes the expansion of Medicaid, increased funding for community health clinics, and an emphasis on culturally competent care.

The struggle for racial justice also extends to the political realm. Liberals strongly advocate for the protection of voting rights, especially for communities of color who have historically faced—and continue to confront—various forms of voter suppression. Policies promoting automatic voter registration, restoring the Voting Rights Act, and opposing discriminatory voter ID laws are central to this effort, ensuring that all voices can be heard in our democracy. Environmental justice is another critical aspect of the liberal approach to racial justice. Recognizing that communities of color are more likely to suffer from environmental hazards, liberals push for stricter regulations on polluting industries and greater investment in clean energy jobs in these communities. They also champion the inclusion of these communities in decision-making processes regarding environmental policies.

On the education front, liberals fight for equal access to quality education for all students, regardless of their racial or ethnic background. This includes increased funding for schools in minority and low-income communities, policies that promote diversity in schools, and the provision of free community college.

Finally, in the economic sphere, liberals seek to close the racial wealth gap through a combination of strategies including increasing the minimum wage, strengthening labor protections, and promoting economic investment in communities of color.

The liberal approach to racial justice and equity is comprehensive, encompassing multiple facets of society. It is rooted in the belief that systemic racism can only be effectively tackled through systemic solutions, and these policy initiatives reflect this perspective. Through these strategies, liberals aim to create an inclusive society where race is no longer a determinant of one's life chances.

As we conclude this exploration of the liberal approach to racial justice and systemic racism, we must remember that the quest for a more equitable society is ongoing. It is not a journey with a clear end point, but a continuous struggle to challenge and dismantle systems of oppression while building more just alternatives in their place.

The future, as envisioned by liberals, is a place where racial and ethnic disparities are not just acknowledged but actively addressed and eliminated. It's a future where systemic racism, in all its forms, is replaced by systemic equality, where every person—regardless of the color of their skin—can fully participate in society and realize their potential.

In the realm of policy, the liberal vision for the future includes more comprehensive and intentional measures to address systemic racism. We can anticipate a continuation of policy initiatives that target racial disparities in areas such as education, housing, healthcare, and criminal justice. Furthermore, there will be a push for innovative strategies, informed by research and community input, to tackle racial inequality.

There will also be a continued emphasis on representation. This means not only advocating for people of color in leadership roles in government, academia, and the private sector, but also ensuring that the voices of marginalized communities are heard and taken into account when designing and implementing policies that affect them.

Finally, the liberal perspective acknowledges that racial justice cannot be achieved in a vacuum. It is intertwined with other forms of social justice—including gender equality, LGBTQ+ rights, economic justice, and environmental sustainability—and all of these issues must be addressed together in order to build a truly equitable society.

While we have come a long way in the struggle for racial justice, there is much work still to be done. The challenges are great, but so too is the liberal commitment to overcoming them. As we look to the future, liberals remain steadfast in their pursuit of a society that is not only diverse, but truly inclusive and equitable—a society where systemic racism has been replaced with systemic justice.

15: International Relations and Diplomacy

In our increasingly interconnected world, effective international relations have become paramount in addressing global challenges and promoting peace. Central to the liberal perspective on global affairs is the firm belief in diplomacy, multilateralism, and global cooperation as cornerstones of international relations. Liberals tend to value the power of dialogue, negotiation, and constructive engagement, favoring these tools over military intervention and isolationist policies. They see the United States not as an autonomous actor in the world stage but as part of a broader, global community, working in concert with other nations to advance mutual interests, uphold human rights, and solve pressing global issues.

This chapter delves into the liberal approach to international relations and diplomacy, elucidating its key principles, goals, and policy preferences. It underscores how a diplomatic and multilateral approach to foreign affairs can foster international cooperation, facilitate conflict resolution, and promote a more peaceful, equitable world.

15.1: Diplomacy and Conflict Resolution

The liberal belief in diplomacy as a tool for conflict resolution is rooted in the understanding that a peaceful dialogue can often yield more productive, lasting results than military action. This approach encourages engagement and negotiation, emphasizing the need to understand and respect differing perspectives, and fostering a climate conducive to problem-solving and cooperation.

Liberals argue that diplomacy enables nations to address the root causes of conflicts rather than merely responding to their consequences, leading to more sustainable peace. Diplomatic initiatives often involve a range of strategies such as mediation, peace talks, and trust-building exercises. They may also involve leveraging international institutions, such as the United Nations or regional bodies, to facilitate negotiation and dialogue.

The Iran Nuclear Deal, also known as the Joint Comprehensive Plan of Action (JCPOA), serves as a prime example of diplomatic conflict resolution. The deal, which was a result of years of diplomatic negotiations, effectively halted Iran's nuclear weapons development program and prevented a potential military confrontation, illustrating the power of diplomacy to resolve international disputes.

Beyond conflict resolution, diplomacy plays a crucial role in maintaining and nurturing relationships with other countries. Liberals advocate for active diplomatic engagement, maintaining embassies and consulates, and employing skilled diplomats who can navigate the intricacies of international relations. They see diplomacy as a way to foster mutual understanding, build alliances, and collaborate on global issues such as climate change, public health crises, and terrorism.

However, it's also recognized that diplomacy requires patience and a long-term vision, as the fruits of diplomatic efforts may not always be immediately apparent. It necessitates a willingness to compromise and a commitment to the principles of international law and respect for the sovereignty of other states.

The liberal emphasis on diplomacy and conflict resolution underscores their commitment to peaceful coexistence, international cooperation, and a world order where disagreements are resolved not on the battlefield, but at the negotiation table.

15.2: Multilateralism and Global Institutions

The liberal commitment to multilateralism is grounded in the belief that cooperation, dialogue, and collective action are vital for addressing the complex and interconnected challenges that the world faces today. This vision of multilateralism is not just about maintaining peace and security, but also about promoting economic development, advancing human rights, and tackling global issues like climate change, pandemics, and poverty.

Multilateralism often manifests through active engagement with global institutions, and liberals value the roles of international organizations such as the United Nations (UN), the World Health Organization (WHO), and the International Monetary Fund (IMF). These organizations are seen as platforms for negotiation and cooperation, providing a framework for collective decision-making and the peaceful resolution of disputes. They also play key roles in setting international norms, monitoring compliance, and providing technical assistance and resources.

The UN, for instance, is highly regarded for its work in maintaining international peace and security, promoting human rights, and coordinating humanitarian assistance. Its agencies, like the WHO, offer technical expertise and coordination in crucial areas such as public health, which was particularly highlighted during the global response to the COVID-19 pandemic.

Similarly, the IMF, the World Bank, and regional development banks are recognized for their role in economic stability and development, offering financial assistance and policy advice to member countries. These institutions, despite criticism and calls for reform, remain at the heart of the liberal vision for a stable, prosperous, and interconnected global economy.

Liberals also value international agreements that set targets and standards for global action. The Paris Climate Accord is one such key agreement, which represents a global commitment to combat climate change and adapt to its effects. Despite criticisms and challenges, the accord is seen as a landmark multilateral effort in the face of one of the world's most pressing challenges.

However, the liberal commitment to multilateralism doesn't imply a blind trust in global institutions or an uncritical acceptance of all their decisions. Rather, it is accompanied by calls for reforms to make these bodies more representative, accountable, and effective. It acknowledges the need for these institutions to evolve and adapt to changing global realities, while remaining central to international cooperation and governance.

The liberal approach to multilateralism and global institutions underscores the belief in collective action, shared responsibility, and global governance in dealing with the world's most pressing challenges.

15.3: Global Cooperation and Human Rights

Global cooperation and human rights sit at the core of the liberal worldview, framing the lens through which liberals approach international relations. It's believed that through collective action and mutual understanding, countries can confront shared challenges, advance common interests, and protect the inherent rights and dignity of all people.

Global cooperation is seen as an essential mechanism for addressing issues that transcend borders. In a world that is increasingly interconnected, problems such as climate change, public health crises, economic instability, and cyber threats demand a collaborative approach. Liberals advocate for countries to work together, share resources, and exchange knowledge to confront these issues effectively.

In the realm of climate change, for example, liberals argue for international collaboration to reduce greenhouse gas emissions, fund renewable energy initiatives, and aid regions most impacted by the adverse effects of climate change. The Paris Climate Agreement stands as a testament to this perspective, signaling a collective global commitment to combat climate change.

Global cooperation is also crucial in the field of public health. The COVID-19 pandemic underscored the necessity for countries to share information, coordinate responses, and ensure equitable access to treatments and vaccines. Liberals support efforts to strengthen international health institutions, such as the World Health Organization, and encourage cooperation in health research, surveillance, and crisis management.

On the economic front, liberals argue for collaboration in maintaining global economic stability, promoting fair trade, and addressing economic inequality. This includes working within frameworks like the World Trade Organization, G7, and G20 to coordinate economic policies, as well as supporting international development through aid and investment in developing nations.

While global cooperation focuses on tackling shared challenges, the commitment to human rights ensures that these efforts uphold the dignity, freedom, and well-being of all individuals. Liberals believe in promoting human rights standards worldwide, advocating for gender equality, racial justice, LGBTQ+ rights, and the rights of indigenous peoples, among others.

In this context, liberals support international human rights instruments like the Universal Declaration of Human Rights and the Human Rights Council. They encourage the international community to hold nations accountable for human rights violations and work towards the eradication of practices such as torture, arbitrary detention, and discrimination.

Global cooperation and the promotion of human rights form the backbone of the liberal approach to international relations. In a world marked by interdependence and shared challenges, liberals believe that nations must work together to build a future that is peaceful, prosperous, and respectful of human dignity.

As we look towards the future, the liberal approach to international relations and diplomacy continues to be shaped by the evolving global landscape. In a world that is increasingly interconnected and interdependent, the principles of diplomacy, multilateralism, global cooperation, and respect for human rights will guide the liberal vision for global peace, prosperity, and justice.

The challenges facing our world are multifaceted and complex, and they require a similarly multifaceted response. Climate change, nuclear proliferation, global pandemics, cyber threats, income inequality—these are all issues that cross borders and impact all countries, regardless of geography or political ideology. As such, they require solutions that are built on a foundation of global cooperation and shared responsibility.

In the face of these challenges, the liberal commitment to diplomacy and negotiation, rather than aggression or unilateralism, remains steadfast. It is believed that maintaining open channels of communication, seeking common ground, and working towards mutually beneficial solutions is the path to peaceful resolution of disputes and global stability.

Moreover, the role of multilateral institutions is more crucial than ever. The United Nations, the World Health Organization, the World Trade Organization, the International Criminal Court, and many others serve not only as platforms for dialogue and cooperation but also as mechanisms for holding states accountable, implementing international law, and making collective decisions.

Last, as we navigate the future, the liberal commitment to human rights serves as a guiding beacon. The struggle for justice, equality, and dignity for all individuals—regardless of race, religion, gender, or sexual orientation—is a struggle that continues to shape the liberal approach to international relations.

The future of international relations under a liberal perspective is one where diplomacy, multilateralism, global cooperation, and respect for human rights form the cornerstones of a more peaceful and just world order. The path may be challenging and fraught with obstacles, but it is one that liberals are committed to treading in pursuit of a better world.

16: Science, Technology, and Innovation

As we move deeper into the 21st century, the influence of science, technology, and innovation on our lives becomes increasingly profound. New discoveries in fields like biotechnology, information technology, renewable energy, and more hold immense potential to improve our world, from the quality of our health to the sustainability of our planet. At the same time, these rapidly evolving domains also present new challenges and ethical questions that must be navigated carefully.

From a liberal perspective, there is a strong commitment to embracing the benefits of science and technological innovation, while also ensuring ethical considerations and human rights are not compromised in the process. Liberals often advocate for policy decisions that are backed by scientific research, ensuring that the course of action we undertake is grounded in facts, not conjecture. They also emphasize the importance of funding research and development, as it is through such initiatives that groundbreaking discoveries are made, and societal progress is achieved.

Furthermore, liberals also focus on bridging the digital divide and protecting digital rights in an era of rapid technological change. They believe that everyone should have equal access to the benefits of technology and that user privacy and data protection should be a priority.

This chapter will delve into these key areas of focus within the liberal stance on science, technology, and innovation. We will explore how the principles of evidence-based policy, research funding, and digital rights play out in the context of current societal challenges and look at how these elements come together in the liberal vision for a future that harnesses the power of science and technology for the betterment of all.

16.1: Promoting Science and Evidence-Based Policy

Science and evidence-based policy stand as cornerstones of the liberal approach to governance. The embrace of science stems from the understanding that policy decisions should be guided by the best available evidence, ensuring that actions taken are rooted in facts and proven effectiveness, rather than political rhetoric or unverified beliefs.

Science plays a pivotal role in the decision-making process across a wide array of policy areas. Climate change, public health, technology, and even economics are all arenas where the liberal commitment to scientific guidance is manifest. For instance, in addressing the COVID-19 pandemic, liberals advocated for policies driven by scientific knowledge about the virus and its spread. Similarly, the liberal stance on climate change is heavily influenced by scientific consensus on the severity of the crisis and the urgent need for action.

The emphasis on science also extends to the advocacy for scientific integrity in public policy. Liberals often voice concern about political interference in scientific research and the dissemination of findings. They champion transparency in how scientific data is used in policy decisions, striving to ensure that research is not misrepresented or suppressed for political purposes.

Moreover, liberals see combating misinformation as a significant part of promoting science. In the digital age, misleading narratives can spread rapidly, leading to public confusion and misguided policy responses. Liberals, therefore, underscore the importance of robust science communication and public education initiatives. This includes efforts to enhance scientific literacy among the public, ensuring that citizens are better equipped to discern valid scientific information from misinformation.

Last, liberals also stress the importance of international scientific cooperation. They believe that global challenges, like climate change or pandemics, require a collaborative scientific response.

This includes sharing research, pooling resources, and coordinating policy responses on a global scale.

The liberal commitment to promoting science and evidence-based policy is grounded in the belief that scientific knowledge is a crucial tool in tackling the most pressing challenges of our time. From advocating for scientific integrity to combating misinformation, liberals envision a policy landscape where decisions are informed by robust, reliable scientific evidence. This dedication to truth and empirical data is a key characteristic of the liberal approach to science, technology, and innovation.

16.2: Funding Research and Development

Research and development (R&D) forms the bedrock of innovation, driving advancements across various sectors from renewable energy to medical technology. Liberals view investment in R&D as a fundamental responsibility of the government, crucial for not only promoting scientific advancement but also for driving economic growth, global competitiveness, and societal well-being.

One of the core areas where liberals advocate for increased R&D funding is in the field of clean energy and environmental technologies. Recognizing the urgent need to transition to a sustainable economy, liberals champion investments in renewable energy sources such as wind and solar power, energy-efficient technologies, and electric vehicles. Funding R&D in these areas is seen as a way to spur innovation, create jobs, and reduce greenhouse gas emissions, aligning economic growth with environmental sustainability.

In the realm of healthcare, liberals stress the need for robust R&D funding to enable breakthroughs in medical science, from novel treatments and therapies to advancements in public health strategies. The COVID-19 pandemic has underscored the importance of rapid and well-funded R&D in responding to global health crises. Liberals, therefore, advocate for strong public investment in health research, as well as policies that encourage private-sector R&D in healthcare.

Furthermore, liberals believe that funding R&D can be a significant driver of economic growth and global competitiveness. Innovation often leads to the creation of new industries and the evolution of existing ones, generating jobs and bolstering the economy. Additionally, being at the forefront of technological innovation can enhance a nation's global standing, ensuring it maintains a competitive edge on the international stage.

Policy initiatives in this regard can take various forms, from direct government funding for scientific research to incentives for private sector R&D. These might include tax credits for businesses engaged in R&D activities, grants for academic institutions, or partnerships between government entities, private businesses, and academic institutions to pool resources and expertise.

Liberals see funding for R&D as a strategic investment in the future. By fueling innovation and enabling scientific advancements, robust R&D funding can help address societal challenges, drive economic growth, and ensure a nation's competitiveness in an increasingly technology-driven global landscape.

16.3: Technological Innovation and Digital Rights

In the digital age, technological innovation has immense potential to transform society, improving productivity, connectivity, and access to information. However, these advancements also raise important questions about digital rights and ethics. In this section, we will examine the liberal approach to fostering innovation while safeguarding these critical rights, covering topics such as net neutrality, privacy protections, the digital divide, and the implications of artificial intelligence and other emerging technologies.

A core principle guiding the liberal perspective on digital rights is net neutrality. Net neutrality is the belief that all internet traffic should be treated equally, with no discrimination or different pricing based on user, content, website, platform, or method of communication. Liberals view net neutrality as essential for maintaining an open internet that fosters innovation and allows for the free exchange of ideas. They argue for robust regulations to prevent Internet Service Providers (ISPs) from throttling, blocking, or prioritizing certain content or services over others.

Privacy rights form another key part of the liberal stance on digital rights. In a world where data has become a valuable commodity, concerns over how personal information is collected, used, and shared have taken center stage. Liberals push for strong data protection laws that empower consumers to control their personal data and hold companies accountable for breaches of privacy.

The digital divide, or the gap between those who have access to modern information technology and those who do not, is another significant concern. Liberals believe in promoting digital inclusivity and reducing this divide by ensuring affordable access to high-speed internet and digital devices for all, regardless of socioeconomic status or geographical location. They see this as a matter of social justice, as well as a necessary step for broad-based economic development.

Finally, the implications of artificial intelligence (AI) and other emerging technologies have risen to the forefront of discussions on technological innovation. As AI becomes increasingly integrated into our daily lives, liberals call for the development of ethical guidelines and regulatory frameworks to guide its use. This includes addressing concerns over algorithmic bias, the impact of automation on jobs, and potential threats to privacy and security.

In short, the liberal approach to technological innovation is centered on harnessing its benefits while ensuring that digital rights and ethical considerations are not overlooked. They advocate for policies that promote a free and open internet, safeguard personal data, reduce the digital divide, and manage the impact of emerging technologies, ensuring that technological progress serves the public interest.

As we look toward the future, the importance of science, technology, and innovation in shaping our world cannot be overstated. Liberals maintain that these fields hold the keys to addressing many of our most pressing challenges, from climate change to public health, economic development, and beyond. In the light of this understanding, they continue to push for policies that foster innovation, prioritize evidence-based decision-making, and uphold the fundamental rights and ethical considerations related to technological advancements.

The frontier of science and technology is always advancing, with emerging fields like AI, quantum computing, synthetic biology, and others continually opening up new possibilities and posing fresh challenges. Navigating this landscape will require careful consideration, informed debate, and responsible stewardship. Liberals insist on the need for a collective commitment to truth, openness, and accountability in this endeavor, emphasizing the importance of public engagement and democratic oversight.

On the policy front, liberals will continue advocating for robust funding for research and development, recognizing the critical role of scientific inquiry and technological innovation in driving economic growth, maintaining global competitiveness, and finding solutions to societal issues. Similarly, they will persist in their efforts to bridge the digital divide, promote net neutrality, and safeguard digital privacy, upholding the principle that access to technology and control over one's digital footprint are fundamental rights in the 21st century.

As we move forward into an increasingly interconnected and technologically sophisticated world, the commitment to these principles will shape not only the landscape of science, technology, and innovation, but also the kind of society we live in. By keeping the focus on ethical, equitable, and inclusive innovation, the liberal approach aims to ensure that the future we build is one that benefits all members of society.

With this belief, the chapter concludes, setting the stage for an enlightened discourse on science, technology, and innovation that continues to evolve with our rapidly changing world. The future holds immense potential and uncertainty, and it is through this liberal lens that we must navigate our path forward.

17: Infrastructure and the Green New Deal

As the world rapidly transforms and faces increasing challenges due to climate change, the need for a renewed approach to infrastructure becomes more evident. Infrastructure, as the underpinning of society, is not merely about physical structures; it's about the systems and services that facilitate our economy's functioning, our communities' connection, and our countries' competitiveness on the global stage. In this chapter, we will explore the liberal vision for a forward-looking, sustainable, and inclusive approach to infrastructure.

Liberals hold the belief that investing in infrastructure is an investment in the country's future, contributing to economic growth, social equity, and environmental sustainability. They envision modernizing and upgrading aging systems, from transportation networks and power grids to water facilities and broadband services. It is seen not just as a response to decaying infrastructure, but also an opportunity to create millions of jobs, reduce inequality, and stimulate local economies.

Moreover, in the context of the escalating climate crisis, the discourse around infrastructure has intertwined with an ambitious proposal—The Green New Deal. This transformative vision seeks to address climate change and economic inequality simultaneously by drastically transforming the country's infrastructure and energy systems. It aims to reduce greenhouse gas emissions, transition to a clean energy economy, and create high-quality jobs, particularly in communities that have been historically disadvantaged.

17.1: Modernizing Infrastructure for the 21st Century

The foundation of a thriving society and robust economy lies in its infrastructure. From the roads we drive on and the bridges we cross to the water we drink and the internet that keeps us connected - infrastructure permeates every aspect of our lives. For liberals, the need for a comprehensive overhaul and modernization of America's infrastructure is not merely an opportunity but a pressing necessity. This recognition drives their commitment to propel the United States into a future where the infrastructure meets the demands of the 21st century and beyond, fostering equitable access, sustainability, and resilience.

First, the state of the transportation infrastructure warrants immediate attention. Aging roads, bridges, and public transit systems not only impair the efficiency and safety of travel but also hinder economic productivity. Liberals propose significant investments in these areas, envisioning a modern transportation network that includes high-speed rail, efficient public transit, and infrastructure for electric vehicles. These initiatives, while reducing congestion and emissions, also have the potential to create millions of jobs.

The water and electrical systems, two critical lifelines of the country, also require upgrades to meet growing needs and challenges. Liberals advocate for replacing lead pipes that taint the water supply, improving water treatment facilities, and increasing the resilience of water systems against climate change. For electrical systems, the focus is on improving grid resilience, promoting energy efficiency, and facilitating the transition to clean energy.

Broadband access, in today's digital age, has emerged as a significant component of infrastructure. The pandemic has underscored the internet's critical role in everything from work and education to healthcare and social connection. Liberals argue for expanding broadband access, particularly in rural and underserved areas, treating it as a public utility that everyone should affordably access.

Importantly, modernizing infrastructure extends beyond mere replacements or upgrades; it involves rethinking design and planning processes to incorporate climate resilience and social equity. This means creating infrastructure that withstands extreme weather events and benefits all communities, including those historically disadvantaged.

Moreover, these investments in infrastructure are not just expenses, but catalysts for economic growth. Job creation is a substantial byproduct of these projects, offering opportunities for workers of different skill levels and sectors. The benefits also ripple through the economy, as improved infrastructure boosts productivity, stimulates local economies, and enhances the nation's global competitiveness.

The path to modernizing America's infrastructure is complex and requires substantial resources. Still, liberals argue that the cost of inaction is far greater, impacting economic growth, social equity, and the nation's capacity to combat climate change. With a forward-looking and inclusive approach, infrastructure modernization could usher in a new era of prosperity and resilience.

17.2: The Green New Deal: Combating Climate Change through Infrastructure

Climate change, arguably the most pressing issue of our time, necessitates bold and transformative action. The liberal response is embodied in the ambitious proposal known as the Green New Deal. Recognizing that the fight against climate change cannot be separated from the infrastructure that underpins our society, the Green New Deal seeks to remodel the American infrastructure landscape, replacing carbon-intensive systems with greener, sustainable alternatives.

The Green New Deal envisages a sweeping transition of the U.S. economy towards clean energy, with an emphasis on renewable sources such as wind, solar, and hydro. This proposal involves substantial investments to upgrade the electrical grid and make it capable of supporting a decentralized, renewable-focused power system. It also calls for the retrofitting and upgrading of buildings across the country to improve energy efficiency and reduce energy consumption, which would contribute significantly to lowering greenhouse gas emissions.

Transportation, being one of the largest sources of carbon emissions, is another crucial focus area in this deal. The Green New Deal calls for a major overhaul of the nation's transportation infrastructure. The vision is to replace fossil fuel-dependent vehicles with electric ones and develop high-speed rail systems as a viable alternative to air travel. Both strategies demand a massive expansion of charging infrastructure and a revamp of the rail network, creating countless jobs in the process.

Simultaneously, the Green New Deal acknowledges the importance of resilience in the face of a changing climate. It proposes investing in climate-resilient infrastructure, particularly in communities most vulnerable to climate impacts. This includes everything from strengthening the flood defenses of coastal communities to improving the fire-resistance of infrastructure in wildfire-prone regions.

The Green New Deal is about more than just infrastructure and climate change, however. It represents a comprehensive and inclusive economic strategy, linking the fight against climate change with job creation and social justice. It advocates for a just transition, ensuring that the shift towards a green economy benefits all communities and creates millions of high-quality jobs.

Critics of the Green New Deal often point to its high cost and ambitious goals. But for its proponents, the costs of inaction far outweigh the costs of action. They argue that it is an investment in our future - a path to a more sustainable, resilient, and equitable society. The Green New Deal represents a reimagining of what infrastructure can and should do: serve as a tool to combat climate change, spur economic growth, and promote social justice. As such, it embodies the liberal conviction that proactive and ambitious policy can mold a better future.

17.3: Economic Growth and Job Creation through Green Infrastructure

The concept of the Green New Deal and the liberal infrastructure plans is not solely confined to environmental sustainability and resilience. At their core, these initiatives also carry enormous economic potential. Through their implementation, they can serve as potent catalysts for economic growth, job creation, and the establishment of new, vibrant industries within the renewable energy sector.

Economic growth, under the banner of these initiatives, comes with an investment focus shift. Traditional forms of energy production and consumption are not only becoming environmentally untenable but also increasingly economically unviable as renewable energy technologies become more affordable and efficient. By investing heavily in renewable energy infrastructure, the U.S. can position itself at the forefront of the global shift towards sustainable energy. This transition paves the way for an era of "green growth," underpinned by industries that are both economically rewarding and environmentally responsible.

The Green New Deal, specifically, proposes a transformative economic stimulus package aiming to address climate change and economic inequality simultaneously. The plan emphasizes job creation, envisioning millions of new jobs in sectors like clean energy production, energy-efficient construction, and sustainable agriculture. In addition to direct job creation, these initiatives would also spur demand in ancillary sectors, resulting in a multiplier effect that could lead to even greater employment growth.

Green infrastructure projects, from installing solar panels and wind turbines to retrofitting buildings for energy efficiency, are labor-intensive undertakings. They require a diverse and substantial workforce spanning a wide range of skills and occupations. Consequently, these projects have the potential to create a significant number of new jobs, particularly in areas hard-hit by the decline of traditional industries like coal mining and manufacturing.

Another salient point is the potential for fostering innovation and competitiveness. By investing in green technologies, the U.S. can stimulate innovation and create a market for new products and services. This innovation, in turn, can enhance the country's global competitiveness, ensuring its position as a leader in the industries of the future.

The economic implications of the Green New Deal and similar infrastructure initiatives go beyond mere numbers. They represent a fundamental shift in how we perceive and value economic growth. Rather than treating economic growth and environmental sustainability as opposing goals, these initiatives present them as mutually reinforcing objectives. They embody a vision of an economy that rewards not just profit, but also sustainability and social justice.

The Green New Deal and liberal infrastructure plans articulate a vision for a green economy that is not only sustainable but also dynamic and inclusive. They signal a recognition that the fight against climate change, if done right, can serve as a significant engine for economic growth and job creation.

As we conclude this exploration of liberal perspectives on infrastructure and the Green New Deal, it's worthwhile to cast our gaze forward and envision the future they propose.

The future, as outlined by these initiatives, is one of resilience and innovation. It pictures an America where infrastructure is no longer a symbol of past glory but a testament to forward-thinking ingenuity and sustainability. High-speed railways, expansive renewable energy grids, and digitally inclusive cities are but a few of the images that come to mind. These are not mere dreams but achievable realities with the right commitment and investment.

This future also promises a renewed economy, reborn in the crucible of green industry and sustainable practices. It's an economy that offers employment and prosperity, not despite its environmental consciousness, but because of it. Through initiatives like the Green New Deal, we could witness a significant uplift in employment across multiple sectors, from renewable energy to green construction. The challenge of climate change, rather than being a burdensome yoke, could instead serve as a springboard for economic revitalization and innovation.

Moreover, this future is one that values social equity and inclusivity. By focusing on job creation and sustainable growth, it ensures that the benefits of this green transition are widely shared. It offers opportunities not just for the few, but for the many, fostering an inclusive economic system that values every contribution.

Yet, this future is by no means guaranteed. It requires persistent effort, considerable investment, and, importantly, collective will. As we move forward, it will be critical to build and maintain momentum for these initiatives. The stakes are high, as is the potential reward. If successful, we stand not only to protect our planet but to create a fairer, more prosperous society.

As we end this chapter, let it serve as a reminder that our future is not something that happens to us—it's something we make. The liberal perspective on infrastructure and the Green New Deal offers a blueprint, but it's up to us to bring that vision to life. The journey may be challenging, but the destination—a sustainable, prosperous, and inclusive America—will undoubtedly be worth it.

18: Affordable Housing and Homelessness

As the wealthiest nation on earth, the United States faces a paradox of abundance amidst deprivation. An increasing number of citizens grapple with housing insecurity and homelessness—a problem that resonates deeply with liberal principles of equity, social justice, and compassion. The reality of families living paycheck to paycheck, individuals residing in substandard housing conditions, or people sleeping on the streets strikes a discordant note in the symphony of American prosperity. As such, addressing these issues becomes not just a matter of economic or social policy, but a question of our collective moral imperative.

The liberal commitment to resolving the affordable housing crisis and combating homelessness is rooted in a belief that everyone deserves a safe, decent, and affordable place to live. Liberals view housing as a human right, not a mere commodity, and believe that no one should be without a home due to economic hardship or systemic inequality. They recognize that the issue is complex and interwoven with numerous other societal challenges, from poverty and racial discrimination to mental health and addiction. Consequently, the approach must be multifaceted, innovative, and persistent, with strategies that range from housing policy reform to direct support services for those experiencing homelessness.

18.1: Tackling the Affordable Housing Crisis

The affordable housing crisis in the United States is a complex and multifaceted issue, marked by a lack of adequate, affordable housing options for a significant proportion of the population. From urban centers to rural towns, the gap between wages and housing costs continues to grow, resulting in a crisis that affects millions of individuals and families. The situation is exacerbated by systemic issues such as racial discrimination, income inequality, and the persistent effects of historical housing policies.

Liberals approach the affordable housing crisis with a sense of urgency, emphasizing the need for robust and comprehensive solutions. One of the fundamental ways to address this issue is through the construction and preservation of affordable housing. To this end, liberals advocate for increasing federal funding for programs such as the Low-Income Housing Tax Credit (LIHTC) and Housing Choice Voucher Program (Section 8), which provide financial incentives for the development of affordable housing and assistance for low-income renters, respectively.

Moreover, liberals champion rent control policies and the establishment of tenants' rights to combat predatory practices and provide stability for renters. By limiting the amount that rents can increase year over year and enacting strong eviction protections, they aim to prevent displacement and homelessness. However, they also recognize the need to balance these regulations with the interests of landlords and housing providers, encouraging a fair and sustainable rental market.

Furthermore, liberals push for fair housing laws and regulations that prevent discriminatory practices based on race, religion, sexual orientation, disability, or family status. They believe that expanding and enforcing these protections is crucial in ensuring equal access to housing and combating historical patterns of segregation and discrimination.

This approach to tackling the affordable housing crisis is rooted in a belief that everyone deserves access to safe, decent, and affordable housing. It highlights the importance of systemic solutions, from increasing the supply of affordable housing and protecting renters to combating housing discrimination. This comprehensive strategy emphasizes that the path to resolving the affordable housing crisis lies not only in addressing immediate housing needs, but also in confronting the larger systemic issues that underpin the crisis.

18.2: Investing in Public Housing and Community Development

Public housing, as a key facet of the social safety net, has a significant role to play in providing affordable and secure living arrangements for those most vulnerable to housing insecurity. However, years of underfunding and neglect have resulted in a public housing system that is often marked by deteriorating buildings, inadequate facilities, and limited availability.

In response to these challenges, liberals underscore the necessity for robust and sustained investment in public housing. They advocate for increased federal funding for the construction, maintenance, and modernization of public housing, stressing the need to reverse the neglect that these communities have faced over the years. Further, they call for measures to ensure that public housing is not only affordable but also safe, healthy, and energy-efficient.

Simultaneously, liberals argue that public housing should not exist in isolation but should be integrated into the wider fabric of the community. They champion the concept of mixed-income housing, which involves the creation of communities that include a blend of market-rate and subsidized housing, fostering greater economic and social diversity.

Moreover, the liberal perspective on housing places a strong emphasis on the role of community development in fostering sustainable, vibrant neighborhoods. Liberals advocate for investment in community resources such as parks, schools, public transportation, and other infrastructure. These investments, they argue, are integral to creating livable neighborhoods and combating the cycle of disinvestment and decline that has historically affected many communities where public housing is located.

Additionally, strategies for sustainable urban development form a key part of the liberal housing agenda. Liberals push for policies that promote the efficient use of land, reduce carbon emissions, and build resilience against the effects of climate change. They view these strategies as essential for ensuring the long-term viability and prosperity of our urban areas.

In essence, the liberal approach to public housing and community development extends beyond simply providing shelter. It seeks to create healthy, sustainable communities that can provide residents with access to the opportunities and resources they need to thrive. The goal is not just affordable housing, but equitable, inclusive neighborhoods that contribute to the wellbeing of all residents.

18.3: Combating Homelessness and Providing Support for Low-Income Families

Homelessness is a pressing social issue that calls for comprehensive, compassionate, and effective solutions. The liberal stance on combating homelessness acknowledges that this is not merely a housing issue—it is intertwined with complex factors such as poverty, unemployment, mental health, and addiction. Thus, addressing homelessness necessitates a multifaceted and interdisciplinary approach.

Liberals place a strong emphasis on prevention strategies and providing robust support for low-income families who are at risk of becoming homeless. They advocate for expanding access to affordable housing and strengthening tenant protections to prevent eviction, which is a leading cause of homelessness. Furthermore, they push for increases in public assistance through programs like the Supplemental Nutrition Assistance Program (SNAP) and Temporary Assistance for Needy Families (TANF), recognizing the role that economic support plays in housing stability.

Homeless veterans and the chronically homeless are two populations that often require specialized services and support. Liberals believe in a 'Housing First' approach for these groups, which prioritizes providing permanent housing as quickly as possible, followed by supportive services like mental health care, substance abuse treatment, and job training. The 'Housing First' approach, which has been shown to be effective in reducing chronic homelessness, reflects the liberal commitment to treating homelessness as a social issue rather than a personal failing.

Furthermore, the liberal approach to combating homelessness emphasizes the importance of wraparound services. These are comprehensive support services designed to help people who are homeless or at risk of homelessness maintain housing and achieve stability in their lives. Wraparound services can include medical and mental health care, job training and placement, financial education, and child care.

Job programs are another important element in the liberal strategy for combating homelessness. Liberals advocate for initiatives that provide job training, employment services, and opportunities for work to people who are homeless or at risk. They argue that employment not only provides income but also contributes to a sense of dignity and self-worth, which can be critical in the journey out of homelessness.

The liberal approach to combating homelessness and supporting low-income families is characterized by its emphasis on prevention, comprehensive support services, and systemic solutions. It is a strategy that recognizes the dignity and potential of every individual and aims to create a society in which everyone has access to safe, stable housing.

As we conclude this exploration of affordable housing and homelessness, it is crucial to consider what the future may hold, and what strategies may lead us toward a more equitable society. Housing, after all, is not merely a commodity—it is a fundamental human right. And yet, it is a right that remains precariously out of reach for far too many individuals.

Today, an unsettling reality haunts our society: nearly everyone is just three bad months away from homelessness. An unexpected medical expense, a lost job, a divorce, or any other life-altering event can quickly deplete savings and push even stable households into the abyss of homelessness. On the flip side, no one is three good months away from becoming a millionaire. It underscores a grim asymmetry in our society, where the descent into poverty can be swift and unexpected, while the climb out of it is slow, often intergenerational, and arduously steep.

But looking to the future, there is room for optimism, hope, and potential change. We have explored the variety of tools in the liberal toolbox—rent control policies, investment in public housing, wraparound services, job programs, and more—that can help combat the affordable housing crisis and homelessness. Each of these solutions, when effectively implemented, has the potential to shift the societal balance, making housing more accessible and less precarious.

The future of housing and homelessness will likely be influenced by a multitude of factors, including policy decisions, economic trends, technological advancements, and societal attitudes. We are in an era of renewed awareness about the extent of inequality and the depth of housing insecurity. A concerted effort that combines policy innovation, public investment, and social compassion could reshape the landscape of housing in America, ensuring that everyone has access to affordable, safe, and stable homes.

Moreover, it is essential to not just focus on immediate solutions but also to address systemic issues that underpin housing insecurity and homelessness. These range from income inequality and job insecurity to healthcare costs and educational opportunities. Addressing these broader issues may take longer and demand more complex and comprehensive solutions, but it is only by doing so that we can make sustainable progress.

As we move forward, let us remember that our society is judged by how it treats its most vulnerable members. As we envision a future where homelessness is a thing of the past, we are reminded of the interconnectedness of our fates. For in creating a society where the precipice of homelessness is not one misstep away for any of us, we build a stronger, more secure foundation for us all.

19: Campaign Finance Reform and Money in Politics

Money and politics have long been intertwined, but the influence of big money in our democratic processes has reached unprecedented levels. This escalating trend raises critical questions about the integrity and inclusiveness of our democracy. As more money flows into the political system, concerns mount about whether politicians are beholden to their constituents or to their wealthiest donors.

In this chapter, we delve into the liberal perspective on campaign finance reform and the necessity of curbing the influence of money in politics. Liberals argue that for the government to truly represent the people, it must be free from the sway of concentrated financial power. It is their belief that every citizen, regardless of their economic status, should have an equal voice in our democracy.

We will explore the impact of landmark rulings such as Citizens United on the political landscape and the rise of Super PACs that have further amplified the voices of the wealthy and well-connected. We will then examine the liberal agenda for reform, which advocates for greater transparency in political donations, limits on campaign contributions, and the public financing of elections as means to restore balance and integrity to our democratic processes.

As we move forward, this chapter aims to shed light on the liberal belief that in order for democracy to flourish, we must ensure that it is not unduly influenced by wealth and that the principles of fairness and equality are upheld in our political sphere.

19.1: The Impact of Money in Politics

The influence of money in American politics cannot be understated. It shapes not only who can run for office but also what issues receive attention and the types of policies that are proposed and implemented. For liberals, this situation presents a profound challenge to the principles of equality and democracy that should underpin our political system.

One aspect of the money-politics dynamic lies in campaign financing. The skyrocketing costs of campaigns, particularly at the federal level, require candidates to raise significant funds. As a result, those who can attract large donors or self-finance have a distinct advantage. This trend has led to a political landscape where the wealthy and well-connected often have more significant influence than average citizens.

This influence extends beyond the election cycle. Donors can wield enormous power over policy, as elected officials may feel compelled to take positions or support legislation that aligns with their donors' interests, consciously or unconsciously. This is especially concerning when the interests of the donors conflict with the needs or desires of the broader populace.

The liberal critique of this system is based on a belief in equal representation – the idea that everyone, regardless of wealth or socioeconomic status, should have an equal say in our democratic processes. They argue that the current campaign finance system undermines this principle, allowing a small group of wealthy individuals and corporations to have a disproportionate impact on policy decisions.

However, the issue is complex and multifaceted, making it essential to understand its depth and breadth. In the following sections, we will delve into the landmark rulings that have shaped the current campaign finance landscape and the proposed solutions that liberals advocate to restore balance to our democracy.

19.2: Citizens United and the Rise of Super PACs

The Supreme Court's 2010 decision in Citizens United v. Federal Election Commission marked a significant turning point in American campaign finance. The ruling held that the First Amendment protects corporations and unions' rights to spend unlimited amounts of money in elections, leading to a dramatic surge in political spending.

For liberals, this decision represents a fundamental threat to democratic representation. They argue that Citizens United opened the floodgates to unchecked spending by corporations and wealthy individuals, drowning out the voices of average citizens and skewing our political system towards the interests of the richest.

One of the most profound impacts of the Citizens United ruling was the rise of Super Political Action Committees (Super PACs). Unlike traditional PACs, Super PACs can raise and spend unlimited sums from corporations, unions, associations, and individuals, though they are prohibited from donating directly to candidates or coordinating with their campaigns. However, this supposed lack of coordination often appears porous, with Super PACs regularly working in parallel with campaign strategies to support favored candidates.

Critics, particularly within liberal circles, argue that Super PACs have exacerbated the issue of money in politics, giving the ultra-wealthy even more power to shape electoral outcomes and policy decisions. They argue that this development undermines democratic principles by allowing a small group of wealthy donors to exert outsized influence over our political system.

For these reasons, many liberals are calling for significant changes to curtail the influence of Super PACs. These include legislative reforms and even a constitutional amendment to overturn Citizens United. In the following section, we will explore these proposed solutions in more detail, examining how liberals hope to reduce the influence of money in politics and restore balance to our democracy.

19.3: The Path to Reform: Public Financing and Transparency

The pervasiveness of money in politics and the challenges it poses to the ideals of a democratic society have prompted liberals to seek fundamental reforms in campaign financing. The ultimate goal is to create a political system where candidates are accountable to the voters, not the highest bidders.

A centerpiece of this reform vision is public financing of elections. Liberals argue that public financing can level the playing field by providing candidates with funds to run competitive campaigns, even if they lack access to wealthy donors or personal wealth. Proponents believe this could not only reduce the influence of big money but also encourage more diverse candidates to run for office, thereby better representing the country's demographic and socioeconomic diversity.

Several models of public financing exist, including matching small donations with public funds, providing vouchers or tax credits for citizens to contribute to campaigns, and offering block grants to candidates who agree to spending limits. Each model has its pros and cons, but all aim to amplify the voices of ordinary citizens and reduce the relative influence of big donors.

In addition to public financing, liberals advocate for greater transparency in campaign funding. They propose stricter reporting requirements for all political donations and spending, including money funneled through Super PACs and dark money groups. The hope is that by shining a light on campaign finance, voters will be better equipped to understand who is trying to influence their votes and why.

Furthermore, transparency can serve as a tool of accountability. If citizens can clearly see who is funding campaigns, they can hold politicians accountable for any potential conflicts of interest or undue influence from special interest groups.

The liberal agenda for campaign finance reform is multifaceted and ambitious. It seeks to restore balance and fairness to a system currently dominated by moneyed interests. With public financing and greater transparency at its core, the path to reform aims to ensure a democracy where the power truly lies in the hands of the people.

As this chapter draws to a close, we cast our eyes towards the future, a future where the promise of democratic participation isn't compromised by the outsized influence of money. The issue of campaign finance reform is one that will continue to be central in American politics, as it strikes at the heart of the nation's democratic ideals.

Liberals, and indeed many conservatives, recognize the need for a system where elections are won based on ideas, integrity, and the ability to represent citizens' needs, not on who can amass the most substantial war chest. They acknowledge that, without reform, the interests of average citizens risk being drowned out by those with the deepest pockets.

Overturning the Citizens United decision, implementing public financing of elections, and increasing transparency in campaign finance are immense challenges. They will require not just legislative and potentially constitutional changes, but also a shift in public understanding and attitudes towards money's role in politics. However, they are challenges that liberals are committed to ftackling head-on in the pursuit of a more equitable democracy.

In the years to come, the battle for campaign finance reform will undoubtedly be a steep uphill climb. Still, it's a battle worth fighting, and one that could dramatically reshape the American political landscape. It's a battle that is fought in the hope of a future where politics is once again the domain of the many, not the few, and where public policy reflects the needs and desires of the citizenry rather than the elite.

In the end, it's a battle for the soul of democracy, where every voice matters, and every citizen, regardless of their financial means, has an equal say in determining the course of the nation. In this future, political power and influence are not commodities to be bought, but responsibilities to be earned.

20. Digital Rights and Net Neutrality

In the twenty-first century, the digital space has become a crucial arena for the exercise of civil rights and liberties. As our lives become increasingly intertwined with the internet and digital technologies, issues of net neutrality, digital rights, and equal access to online services have taken center stage in the public discourse. This chapter delves into the liberal perspective on these issues, showcasing a commitment to safeguarding the internet as an open, equitable, and secure platform for all.

Net neutrality—the principle that all internet traffic should be treated equally—forms the backbone of a free and fair online ecosystem, preventing internet service providers from manipulating speed, access, or cost based on content. Furthermore, as the internet has become a repository of personal information, digital rights, and online privacy have emerged as critical facets of modern civil rights, urging us to reconsider the frameworks of protection for the digital citizen. Last, the digital divide, or the gap between those who have ready access to computers and the internet and those who do not, poses a significant challenge in realizing the ideal of universally accessible online services.

Together, these topics reflect the multifaceted approach required to navigate the complex terrain of digital policy, as we strive to balance progress, protection, and access in the digital age. The following sections will elucidate the liberal commitment to protecting net neutrality, championing digital rights, and bridging the digital divide.

20.1: The Importance of Net Neutrality

Net neutrality is a concept that stipulates that all internet traffic should be treated equally by Internet Service Providers (ISPs). This principle prohibits ISPs from speeding up, slowing down, or blocking any content, applications, or websites, ensuring that users have equal access to all information on the internet. This commitment to a free and open internet has become a cornerstone of liberal policy in the digital era.

In the view of liberals, net neutrality is integral to preserving the internet as a democratic space where every voice has an equal chance to be heard. It facilitates innovation by allowing startups and small businesses to compete on an even playing field with established companies. Without net neutrality, large corporations could potentially pay ISPs for faster internet speeds, creating a 'fast lane' for those who can afford to pay while relegating others to 'slow lanes.'

Moreover, net neutrality prevents censorship, ensuring that ISPs can't block or slow down content based on its message or source. This protects freedom of speech, an essential democratic value, in the digital space.

In recent years, the debate around net neutrality has heated up, with several attempts to dismantle these protections. Liberals argue that such moves would hand control of the internet over to corporate interests at the expense of consumers and small businesses. Consequently, liberals continue to fight to uphold and codify net neutrality laws, considering it as a fundamental aspect of a free, fair, and accessible internet.

This unwavering commitment to net neutrality underscores the broader liberal perspective on digital policy—one where fairness, access, and freedom from corporate monopolization form the guiding principles. In the next sections, we will explore how these principles translate to issues of digital rights and the digital divide.

20.2: Digital Rights and Online Privacy

In an era where much of our lives are conducted online, the protection of digital rights and online privacy has taken center stage in liberal policy considerations. This section explores these concerns, highlighting the liberal commitment to safeguarding personal data and advocating for a more equitable digital environment.

To liberals, the right to privacy extends to the digital sphere. Every internet user should have control over their personal data and how it is collected, stored, and used. The increasing consolidation of data by tech giants and the commodification of personal information, often dubbed 'surveillance capitalism,' is seen as a major challenge to this right.

From targeted advertising to potential breaches of sensitive information, the misuse of personal data poses a significant threat to individual privacy and autonomy. Liberals argue that the unregulated accumulation and exploitation of personal data by companies can lead to manipulation, discrimination, and breaches of trust.

Moreover, there are concerns about government surveillance and potential infringements on civil liberties. The balance between security and privacy is a delicate one, and liberals advocate for stringent checks and balances to prevent overreach and protect citizens' rights.

To address these challenges, liberals push for robust legislation that enshrines digital rights and online privacy. This includes data protection laws that give individuals more control over their personal information, measures to ensure transparency in how data is used, and regulations to prevent the abuse of personal data by both private companies and public authorities.

In addition to privacy, digital rights also encompass issues like freedom of expression, access to information, and net neutrality. By upholding these rights, liberals aim to create an online environment where people can freely express themselves, access information, and participate in digital society without fear of unwarranted intrusion or manipulation.

In the following section, we will further explore how the commitment to digital rights plays into larger discussions about digital access and the digital divide.

20.3: The Digital Divide and Internet Access for All

As we delve deeper into the Information Age, access to the internet has become as essential as access to other basic services like water and electricity. However, a significant digital divide persists, which separates those who have easy, reliable access to the internet and digital technology from those who do not. This section delves into this issue, focusing on the liberal commitment to bridging this divide and ensuring universal internet access.

The digital divide is not merely a global issue between technologically advanced and developing nations; it's also a pressing domestic concern. Both urban and rural areas in the United States suffer from inadequate internet access. In urban environments, the issue often revolves around affordability, with low-income households struggling to afford high-speed internet services. In rural areas, the challenge often lies in the lack of infrastructure, as many areas are not served by internet service providers.

Liberals view the digital divide as an issue of equity and social justice. As more essential services and opportunities move online - from education to job applications to healthcare - lack of internet access effectively excludes certain populations from these opportunities, exacerbating social and economic inequalities.

To address this, liberals advocate for significant investment in digital infrastructure and the promotion of policies that ensure internet access is affordable and accessible for all. This may involve subsidies for low-income households, regulations to ensure fair pricing, or public broadband initiatives to serve areas that are not profitable for private providers.

In addition, there's a liberal focus on digital literacy. It's not enough to just provide the infrastructure and access; people also need the skills to navigate the digital world effectively and safely. Therefore, digital literacy programs are seen as an essential part of the strategy to bridge the digital divide.

By ensuring universal internet access, liberals aim to create a more equitable society where everyone has the tools and opportunities to succeed in the digital age. This vision aligns with the broader liberal commitment to digital rights, which we have explored in this chapter. As we conclude, we will look towards a future where these rights are protected and universally accessible, creating a digital landscape that empowers all individuals and serves as a force for good in society.

As we conclude this exploration of net neutrality and digital rights, the liberal vision for the future is one where the internet remains a vibrant, open space that fuels innovation, fosters democracy, and ensures access to information for all.

Net neutrality will continue to be a core issue as we move forward. The liberal vision for the future seeks a world where internet service providers do not discriminate between different kinds of content or services, allowing a free and open internet that guarantees equal opportunities for all users.

The future also holds challenges and opportunities in ensuring digital rights and online privacy. As technology continues to advance, so do the complexities of privacy and data security.

Liberals will strive to update legislation and regulations to keep pace with technological change and protect users in the digital space. They will continue pushing for transparency from tech companies, and champion initiatives that give individuals more control over their personal data.

Finally, addressing the digital divide remains a crucial goal for the future. The hope is for a society where everyone, regardless of their geographic location or economic status, has equal access to the digital world. This vision involves significant investment in infrastructure, public policy changes, and continued efforts in education to boost digital literacy.

In this future, the internet is not a luxury or a commodity, but a right that is available to all. The fight for net neutrality, digital rights, and universal access represents a fight for a more inclusive, equitable society. These issues will undoubtedly continue to be at the forefront of liberal policy as we navigate the increasingly digital future.

21: Mental Health and Substance Abuse

Mental health and substance abuse issues are ubiquitous, affecting millions of people across the United States. The repercussions extend beyond individual suffering, with significant societal costs in terms of healthcare expenditures, reduced productivity, and burdened criminal justice systems. Nevertheless, these issues are frequently underdiscussed, misunderstood, and stigmatized, impeding the progress of effective prevention and treatment strategies.

In this chapter, we will delve into the liberal perspective on mental health and substance abuse, a perspective that underscores the necessity for compassionate, evidence-based, and comprehensive approaches. Liberal policies and advocacy in this realm are predicated on the belief that mental health is an integral part of overall health and that our society should dedicate substantial resources to address these issues effectively. This includes enhancing funding and access to mental health services, reducing stigma and fostering mental health awareness, and adopting a public health approach towards substance abuse encompassing prevention, treatment, and decriminalization.

21.1: Increasing Funding and Access to Mental Health Services

The liberal perspective strongly endorses the need for increased funding and access to mental health services. This commitment is anchored in the recognition that mental health issues are just as consequential as physical health problems, warranting equal attention, funding, and accessibility in healthcare provision.

Underfunding and neglect of mental health services have been pervasive issues in the United States, contributing to significant unmet needs among those suffering from various mental health disorders. Liberals argue that this gap should be bridged by allocating more public funds towards mental health services, thereby improving the capacity and quality of care available.

Simultaneously, liberal policy makers emphasize the importance of broadening insurance coverage for mental health treatment. The implementation of the Affordable Care Act (ACA) was a significant step in this direction, mandating insurance providers to cover mental health services just as they would physical health services. However, liberals contend that more needs to be done to ensure that everyone, regardless of income, employment status, or geographical location, can afford and access mental health services when needed.

Furthermore, the integration of mental health care into primary care settings is a priority in the liberal agenda. This approach allows for the early identification and treatment of mental health issues, helping to prevent the escalation of these conditions. It also reduces stigma by normalizing mental health care as a regular part of health care.
Finally, liberals are committed to addressing the disparities in access to mental health services across various populations. This includes efforts to reach rural communities, where mental health services are often scarce, and marginalized groups, such as racial and ethnic minorities, the LGBTQ+ community, veterans, and the homeless, who face unique barriers to accessing mental health care.

Overall, the liberal perspective on increasing funding and access to mental health services revolves around the belief that mental health care is a right, not a privilege, and it's imperative that the societal structures reflect this conviction.

21.2: Reducing Stigma and Promoting Mental Health Awareness

The liberal perspective recognizes the profound role that stigma plays in exacerbating mental health issues and impeding access to necessary treatment. Consequently, it champions initiatives aimed at reducing this stigma and promoting mental health awareness.

Stigma, or the negative attitudes and discrimination towards people with mental health disorders, can manifest in numerous ways, from social exclusion to employment discrimination. This stigma can deter individuals from seeking help, further isolating them and worsening their conditions. The liberal approach to tackling this issue is multifaceted and includes public education initiatives, changes in workplace policies, and legislative measures.

Public education initiatives are seen as vital tools to increase awareness about mental health issues, dispel myths, and promote understanding and empathy. Liberals advocate for mental health education in schools and community settings, as well as in media representations, to normalize discussions around mental health and present accurate portrayals of mental illness.

In the workplace, liberals push for policies that create a supportive environment for employees dealing with mental health issues. This includes implementing mental health training for managers, offering comprehensive mental health benefits, and providing accommodations for employees in need.

From a legislative perspective, liberals support measures that protect individuals with mental health disorders from discrimination. The enforcement of the Americans with Disabilities Act (ADA), which includes mental illnesses as a form of disability, and the mental health parity laws are key parts of this approach.

By advancing these initiatives, liberals aim to create a society where mental health is openly discussed, understood, and supported. They envision a future where stigma no longer presents a barrier to treatment, and individuals with mental health issues are accepted and valued in their communities.

21.3: Addressing Substance Abuse: Prevention, Treatment, and Decriminalization

In the face of the ongoing substance abuse crisis, liberals advocate for a comprehensive public health approach that prioritizes prevention, treatment, and decriminalization over punitive measures.

The first pillar of this approach is prevention. Liberals believe in the implementation of community-based prevention programs that aim to reduce risk factors and enhance protective factors related to substance abuse. Such initiatives might include education about the dangers of substance misuse, mentorship programs for at-risk youth, and community efforts to change social norms around drug use.

When it comes to treatment, liberals argue for increased access to evidence-based treatment options. This involves removing barriers to treatment such as high costs, lack of insurance coverage, or geographical obstacles. It also means supporting research into the most effective treatment methodologies, training healthcare providers in these methods, and integrating substance abuse treatment with other healthcare services.

Last, many liberals support the decriminalization of certain substances as a means of reducing the harms associated with substance abuse and the War on Drugs. Decriminalization involves shifting the focus from criminal penalties for substance possession to a health-centered approach. By treating substance abuse as a health issue rather than a criminal one, liberals argue that we can reduce the stigma associated with substance abuse, lessen the burden on the criminal justice system, and better support individuals in overcoming their substance use issues.

Underpinning all of these measures is the belief that everyone deserves compassion, support, and access to effective treatment in the face of substance abuse. By advocating for a more holistic, health-centered approach, liberals aim to create a future where society responds to substance abuse with understanding and care rather than judgment and punishment.

As we look to the future, the liberal vision for addressing mental health and substance abuse involves a society in which stigma is replaced with understanding, punitive measures are replaced with compassion, and barriers to care are dismantled to allow equitable access to treatment.

In the realm of mental health, the hope is for a future where mental health services are readily accessible, fully funded, and integrated into standard healthcare systems. Public education initiatives would be widespread, ensuring that mental health literacy is common knowledge, thus helping to reduce stigma. The working world would adapt to be more accommodating of mental health needs, with robust workplace mental health policies becoming the norm.

When it comes to substance abuse, the future lies in shifting the current punitive paradigm to one that views substance abuse as a public health issue rather than a criminal one. This approach advocates for policies that emphasize prevention, provide access to comprehensive treatment services, and support recovery. As the perspective on substance abuse evolves, it's hoped that decriminalization of certain substances may also become part of the broader societal approach, lessening the burden on the criminal justice system and focusing resources on treatment and recovery.

This forward-looking vision reflects the liberal dedication to fostering a society that supports the well-being of all its members. It's a world where mental health and substance abuse are recognized as crucial components of public health, addressed not with judgement and punishment, but with understanding, compassion, and evidence-based care. While there are challenges on the horizon, the goal remains clear: to create a society in which every individual has the support they need to thrive mentally and physically.

22: Arts and Culture Funding

The arts and culture are vital components of a thriving society, not only as a testament to human creativity and expression but also as contributors to economic growth, education, and community vitality. Liberals believe in the inherent value of the arts, recognizing their transformative power to challenge perspectives, foster dialogue, and build bridges across diverse communities. Government involvement in supporting the arts is therefore seen not as an optional extra but as a fundamental investment in the enrichment and well-being of society.

This chapter delves into the liberal perspective on the importance of arts and culture funding. It discusses the multi-faceted role of the arts in society, the mechanisms through which the government can provide support, and the significance of broad access to and education in the arts. Through these discussions, we hope to illuminate the liberal viewpoint on why arts and culture matter, and how they should be nurtured in a progressive society.

22.1: The Role of Arts and Culture in Society

Arts and culture play a significant role in shaping and reflecting society. They allow us to express our values, challenge norms, foster creativity, and build bridges across diverse communities. Liberals recognize these diverse roles that arts and culture play in our lives, from enhancing our understanding of the world around us to contributing to our overall quality of life.

From a socio-cultural perspective, arts and culture provide a platform for the expression of ideas, emotions, and experiences that transcend language barriers. They foster empathy, understanding, and social cohesion by enabling people to share and experience diverse perspectives. They are also vital in preserving historical narratives and cultural heritage, allowing societies to remember, understand, and learn from their past.

From an economic perspective, the creative sector contributes significantly to employment and economic growth. It spurs innovation, attracts tourism, and enhances the attractiveness of communities as places to live and work. Investing in the arts thus contributes to broader economic development and prosperity.

In the realm of education, arts and culture are seen as essential components of a comprehensive education. They foster creativity, critical thinking, and problem-solving skills, which are increasingly important in the 21st-century workforce. Additionally, exposure to arts education has been linked to improved academic performance, higher graduation rates, and enhanced social-emotional development among students.

The liberal viewpoint asserts that recognizing and promoting the manifold benefits of arts and culture is integral to the development of a vibrant, inclusive, and innovative society. Thus, it is a governmental responsibility to ensure that these sectors receive the necessary support and protection to thrive. The next sections will delve deeper into the mechanisms for this support and the specific policies that liberals advocate to sustain and enhance arts and culture in our society.

22.2: Government Funding for the Arts and Creative Industries

Public funding for the arts and creative industries is a cornerstone of liberal policy, reflecting a commitment to fostering cultural expression, enhancing accessibility, and promoting economic growth. This section will explore the importance of such funding, the various mechanisms through which it is provided, and how these investments stimulate the broader creative economy.

Government funding for the arts typically comes in many forms, including direct funding, grants, endowments, and tax incentives. Direct funding often goes towards supporting public arts institutions, such as museums, theatres, and orchestras, as well as funding arts education in schools. Grants are typically used to support individual artists, small arts organizations, and community arts projects. Endowments help to ensure the long-term financial stability of cultural institutions, while tax incentives encourage private sector investment in the arts.

Public broadcasting is another crucial aspect of government funding for the arts and culture. Public radio and television stations provide a platform for creative content that might not otherwise find a place in the commercial market. These outlets can offer programming that focuses on cultural enrichment, education, and public affairs, fulfilling a public service remit that goes beyond pure entertainment.

Moreover, government funding plays a significant role in promoting equity within the arts. By providing resources for community-based arts initiatives, underserved populations, and marginalized artists, public funding can help ensure a more diverse and inclusive arts landscape.

Investment in the arts and creative industries also stimulates the broader economy. The creative sector is a significant contributor to economic growth and employment. It not only provides jobs within the sector but also supports ancillary businesses, from suppliers to hospitality and tourism. By fostering innovation and creativity, a thriving arts sector can also enhance a nation's global competitiveness.

Critics might argue that public funding for the arts is a luxury, particularly in times of budgetary constraint. However, from a liberal perspective, such funding is seen not as a luxury, but as a necessity—an investment in the cultural, educational, and economic fabric of society. The final section will further delve into the specific liberal policies aimed at bolstering this vital sector.

22.3: Advocacy for Greater Arts Education and Access

Arts education and accessibility are critical tenets of liberal arts policy, reflecting a belief that cultural experiences are integral to personal growth, societal cohesion, and democratic participation. This section examines the commitment to arts education, the importance of preserving cultural heritage, and the role of public institutions in making arts and culture accessible to all.

Arts education is more than just an additional subject in the curriculum; it's a catalyst for creativity, critical thinking, and empathy. Liberals advocate for comprehensive arts education in public schools, not only to foster artistic talent but also to equip students with vital skills for the future. Arts education encourages self-expression, promotes cultural understanding, and can often serve as a gateway to academic engagement for students who might otherwise feel disengaged from traditional educational tracks.

Beyond the classroom, community-based arts programs and extracurricular activities provide additional avenues for artistic exploration and growth, serving to supplement school-based programming. Such initiatives can provide meaningful cultural experiences, fostering community engagement and lifelong learning.

Preserving and enhancing access to cultural heritage is another crucial facet of liberal arts policy. Public museums, libraries, and cultural institutions serve as custodians of cultural heritage, providing invaluable resources for education and research. Liberals argue for robust funding for these institutions to ensure they can fulfill their mandates and remain accessible to all, regardless of economic status.

Accessibility goes beyond physical access. Liberals also champion initiatives that make the arts more inclusive and representative, such as supporting diverse artists, showcasing underrepresented voices, and developing outreach programs for marginalized communities. The digital age also brings new opportunities and challenges for accessibility, with liberals advocating for digital inclusivity and ensuring the digital divide does not restrict access to online cultural content.

The liberal commitment to arts education and accessibility reflects a belief in the democratization of culture. It's based on the understanding that everyone, regardless of background or income, should have the opportunity to participate in, create, enjoy, and benefit from the arts. The final section will look forward to the future of arts and culture from a liberal perspective.

Looking forward, the future of arts and culture within the liberal perspective is one of continued advocacy, adaptation, and evolution. As society changes, so too must our approach to supporting and integrating the arts and culture. Liberals envision a future where the arts are woven seamlessly into the fabric of everyday life, contributing to vibrant, diverse, and inclusive communities.

In terms of public funding, the liberal perspective calls for sustained and enhanced investment in the arts and creative industries. As the economic value of the creative sector continues to grow, so will the necessity for supportive government policies. This includes not only direct funding but also tax incentives, infrastructure development, and other mechanisms that encourage artistic innovation and cultural entrepreneurship.

Education will remain a key battleground in the fight for a more culturally enriched society. Liberals will continue to push for comprehensive arts education in public schools, arguing that exposure to arts and culture is a critical component of well-rounded student development. Moreover, they will champion the cause of lifelong learning, emphasizing that opportunities to engage with the arts should not end after formal education.

Accessibility and inclusivity will also be pivotal in shaping the future of arts and culture policy. In a world that is increasingly digital, the liberal agenda will undoubtedly continue to tackle the challenge of the digital divide in access to cultural content. Efforts will be made to ensure that everyone can benefit from the digital revolution in arts and culture, regardless of their socioeconomic status.

Further, there will be an ongoing commitment to make arts and culture more reflective of societal diversity. This includes championing diverse voices in the arts, ensuring equitable representation in cultural institutions, and making conscious efforts to engage underserved and marginalized communities.

The liberal vision for the future of arts and culture is one of inclusion, accessibility, and vibrancy. It's a vision that sees the arts not as a luxury, but as a necessity, integral to personal growth, community well-being, and societal progress. The commitment is to create a future where everyone can participate in, benefit from, and be enriched by a thriving cultural landscape.

23: Copyright Reform and Creative Commons

In an era defined by the rapid flow of information and digital connectivity, the role of copyright law and the concept of creative ownership are more relevant than ever. As stewards of innovation, creativity, and access to knowledge, liberals consider copyright reform as a necessary and urgent dialogue. Balancing the rights of creators to benefit from their work with the public's access to knowledge and culture is a complex task, fraught with legal and ethical considerations.

This chapter discusses the liberal approach to copyright reform, recognizing that laws conceived in an age of physical media may not suitably translate to the digital realm. The emphasis is on ensuring that copyright law encourages creativity and innovation, rather than stifling it. Further, it highlights the liberal commitment to making cultural and intellectual resources accessible to all, not just those who can afford it.

We also delve into the Creative Commons movement, an innovative alternative that allows creators to share their works more openly and collaboratively. By fostering a digital environment where knowledge and creativity can flow more freely, liberals believe that we can cultivate a more informed, vibrant, and equitable society. The sections that follow detail these aspects in greater depth, from the need for balance in copyright laws to the values inherent in the open culture movement.

23.1: The Balance in Copyright: Creators' Rights and Public Access

Copyright law, at its core, aims to strike a delicate balance. On one hand, it must protect the rights of creators, ensuring they can receive due recognition and reap financial benefits from their creations. On the other hand, it must ensure that the public can access, learn from, and build upon these works, advancing societal knowledge and culture. As we transition further into the digital age, liberals believe that this balance is increasingly important - and challenging - to maintain.

From the liberal perspective, robust copyright protections are necessary to foster a thriving creative economy. Artists, writers, filmmakers, and other creators should have the security of knowing that their original works will not be unfairly exploited. Such protection not only validates their creative endeavors but also provides a critical economic incentive for the production of new and diverse works.

However, it's equally important to ensure that copyright law does not become a barrier to the public's access to knowledge and culture. Overly stringent protections could limit the spread of ideas, restrict artistic expression, and stifle innovation. This is especially concerning in the digital age, where remixing, repurposing, and sharing content have become integral parts of cultural exchange and creativity.

Liberals advocate for copyright reform that respects creators' rights but also acknowledges the importance of fair use, which allows limited use of copyrighted material without permission for purposes such as criticism, news reporting, teaching, and research. They also support measures to ensure that copyright terms do not extend unnecessarily beyond the creator's lifetime, thereby limiting public access to culturally significant works.

The path to reform involves a careful reevaluation of current laws, a process that must be guided by the twin objectives of promoting creativity and ensuring public access to works of art and knowledge. Through dialogue, legislation, and cooperation with creators and consumers, liberals believe that a more balanced and effective copyright system can be achieved.

23.2: The Need for Copyright Reform

The world we live in is rapidly changing, spurred on by developments in digital technology and the internet. However, copyright law, established in a time of tangible and static mediums, often struggles to keep pace with these changes. From a liberal perspective, there is a pressing need for copyright reform that can adapt to the evolving digital landscape, maintaining the critical balance between creators' rights and public access.

One area of concern is the duration of copyright terms. Currently, U.S. copyright law provides protection for the life of the author plus 70 years, or 95 years for corporate authors. These lengthy terms, initially intended to allow creators and their families to benefit from the works, have come under scrutiny. Critics argue that such prolonged protection may restrict public access and use of cultural and intellectual works far longer than necessary. For instance, the continued copyright protection of works from authors long deceased arguably does little to incentivize new creativity. Liberals advocate for a reexamination of these terms, with a view to a possible reduction or the implementation of a renewal system, ensuring protection is still desired and relevant.

The digital age has also introduced new challenges to copyright enforcement. The ease of copying and distributing content online has resulted in widespread infringement, often leaving individual creators and small businesses powerless against the onslaught of piracy. Conversely, excessive enforcement measures could stifle creativity and impede the free flow of ideas and knowledge, which are central to a thriving internet culture.

Reform in the digital context might involve refining the definition of fair use and making it more applicable to the digital environment, clarifying the responsibilities of online service providers, and devising enforcement measures that are proportionate and respect users' rights.

Finally, the existing copyright law is complex and often inaccessible to the public, creators, and small businesses. The liberal view argues for a more transparent and user-friendly system. This could involve simplifying legal language, providing better resources for understanding copyright law, and ensuring the law works for all parties involved, not just large corporations and publishing houses. Liberals view copyright reform as an opportunity to make the system more balanced, flexible, and reflective of our contemporary digital society. By doing so, it can continue to serve its dual purposes: protecting creators and promoting public access to culture and knowledge.

23.3: Creative Commons and Open Culture

In a world where the Internet and digital technologies have revolutionized how we create, share, and consume content, traditional copyright models are increasingly coming under scrutiny. Emerging from this dynamic context, Creative Commons and the broader open culture movement represent promising alternatives that align with the liberal values of accessibility, openness, and collaboration.

Creative Commons is a non-profit organization that provides free, easy-to-use copyright licenses that allow creators to legally share their works with the public. Rather than an "all rights reserved" approach, these licenses operate on a "some rights reserved" basis. Creators can choose how others may use their work, allowing for possibilities like adaptation, remixing, commercial use, and more, while still retaining their copyright.

These licenses are a powerful tool in fostering an open culture – a culture that values the freedom to use, distribute, and modify creative works, within the boundaries set by the creator. This can lead to increased collaboration, innovation, and access to knowledge and culture, which is at the heart of the liberal perspective on copyright.

In practical terms, the impact of Creative Commons and the open culture movement can be seen across various sectors. In education, open educational resources (OERs) that are freely accessible and customizable have transformed teaching and learning. In the arts, musicians, photographers, and artists use Creative Commons licenses to reach wider audiences and invite creative collaboration. In research, open access publications make scholarly articles available to the public, promoting transparency and knowledge dissemination.

Yet, while these movements have made significant strides, there are challenges to overcome. These include raising awareness about Creative Commons and open culture, addressing concerns about quality control and misuse of works, and navigating the complexities of international copyright law.

From a liberal perspective, the evolution and adoption of these alternative models should be encouraged, ensuring that our digital culture continues to be a space for creativity, collaboration, and democratic access to knowledge. The advancement of Creative Commons and open culture not only supports individual creators but also enriches the public domain, leading to a more vibrant, innovative, and inclusive society.

As we gaze into the future, the potential of the digital age in shaping copyright laws and creative freedom is immense. In light of this, the liberal agenda's commitment to copyright reform and the promotion of Creative Commons and open culture becomes even more critical. While traditional copyright law has served an important function in safeguarding the rights of creators, it is clear that these laws must continue to evolve and adapt to keep pace with the rapid technological advances that characterize our age. This is particularly important as we witness the emergence of new forms of creative expression that blur the lines between creators and consumers. In this landscape, ensuring that copyright laws facilitate, rather than stifle, creativity and access to culture is of paramount importance.

Similarly, the Creative Commons and open culture movements will continue to play a crucial role in shaping the future of creativity and knowledge sharing. Their ethos of collaboration and accessibility aligns perfectly with the digital age's ethos, where barriers to creating and sharing content are continuously being reduced.

However, there will be challenges ahead. As more and more people around the world gain access to digital technologies, ensuring that they are aware of their rights as creators and consumers of content is crucial. The goal should be to foster a culture that values and respects these rights, while also embracing the spirit of openness and collaboration.

Ultimately, the liberal vision for the future of copyright reform and creative commons is one that balances the rights of creators with the needs of the public, fostering an environment where creativity, culture, and knowledge can flourish for all. In this future, copyright is not a barrier but a facilitator of creativity and cultural exchange, and the Internet remains an open platform for innovation, learning, and collaboration. This vision is not only achievable but essential for the enrichment of society in the digital age and beyond.

24: Patent Reform and Innovation

In an increasingly globalized and technologically advanced world, innovation is the engine that drives economic growth and societal progress. At the heart of this process is the patent system, designed to encourage new inventions by granting inventors exclusive rights to their creations for a limited period of time. However, like any system, it requires careful balancing and constant updating to ensure that it continues to serve its intended purpose effectively.

The liberal perspective on patent reform aims to strike a balance between incentivizing innovation and ensuring healthy competition. Liberals generally agree that while patent protection is vital for motivating research and development, excessive patent monopolies and the practices of so-called "patent trolls" can stifle innovation and limit access to new technologies.

In this chapter, we delve into the challenges and opportunities associated with patent reform. We explore the essential role of patents in fostering innovation and economic growth, the issues arising from the current patent system, and the liberal vision for a balanced, future-oriented patent system that promotes both innovation and competition. The chapter also examines the critical role of government in supporting research and development, and the importance of maintaining a robust and fair patent system for the overall health of the economy and society.

24.1: The Role of Patents in Innovation and Economic Growth

Patents play an indispensable role in driving innovation and economic growth. By providing inventors with a temporary monopoly on their creations, the patent system incentivizes the significant investments of time, money, and effort required to develop new technologies and processes. This has the potential to result in a dynamic, innovative economy, with a constant flow of new goods, services, and technologies.

From a liberal perspective, patents are seen as a necessary element of the innovation ecosystem. They provide the crucial protection that inventors need to pursue their innovations, facilitating the technological progress that underpins economic development and societal advancement. In many ways, patents are viewed as a social contract between inventors and society. In exchange for a period of exclusivity, inventors agree to disclose their invention, which subsequently becomes part of the public domain and a foundation for further innovation.

However, liberals also recognize the need for balance. While granting temporary monopolies through patents can spur innovation, these monopolies should not be so expansive as to stifle competition or limit access to beneficial technologies. Striking this balance is a key concern for liberals, who advocate for a patent system that encourages innovation while also ensuring that inventions are eventually accessible to all, contributing to a broad-based, inclusive economy.

In this context, the role of government is critical. Public policy can shape the patent system in ways that both reward inventors and safeguard the public interest. It can ensure that the duration and scope of patents are calibrated to stimulate innovation without unduly limiting competition and accessibility. It can also provide direct support for research and development, complementing the incentives provided by patents.

The next sections will delve further into these issues, examining the challenges facing the current patent system and the liberal approach to patent reform.

24.2: The Problem with Patent Trolls and Excessive Patent Monopolies

While the patent system serves a crucial role in promoting innovation, it is not without its flaws. Two of the most prominent issues facing the current system are the phenomena of patent trolls and excessive patent monopolies.

Patent trolls, more formally known as Non-Practicing Entities (NPEs), are companies that acquire patents not to develop new products or technologies, but to profit from licensing fees or litigation against alleged infringers. These entities have been a contentious issue in the world of patent law, as their practices can deter innovation and impose significant costs on productive companies.

Excessive patent monopolies, on the other hand, refer to situations where patents are overly broad or their duration is excessively long, restricting competition and limiting access to valuable technologies. This not only inhibits other innovators from building upon existing ideas but also keeps prices high for consumers and stifles technological progress.

From a liberal standpoint, these issues are of major concern. The liberal philosophy places a high value on competition, innovation, and accessibility - all of which are undermined by patent trolls and excessive patent monopolies. In stifling competition and innovation, these practices are seen to be inhibiting economic growth and social progress.

Therefore, liberals advocate for reforms to tackle these issues. This includes measures such as improving patent quality to reduce the incidence of overly broad or weak patents, adjusting patent terms to prevent excessive monopolies, and implementing legal and policy changes to discourage the practices of patent trolls.

In the next section, we'll examine some of these proposed reforms in greater detail, exploring how they align with the liberal commitment to fostering a vibrant, competitive, and inclusive innovation ecosystem.

24.3: The Path to Patent Reform: Promoting Innovation and Competition

The liberal perspective on patent reform is grounded in the belief that a balanced and fair patent system is key to promoting innovation, supporting economic growth, and ensuring healthy competition. Liberals advocate for comprehensive patent reform that addresses key issues like patent trolls and excessive patent monopolies while fostering an environment conducive to innovation.

A primary focus of liberal patent reform is curbing the activities of patent trolls. This could involve changes to patent litigation practices to discourage the filing of frivolous lawsuits. Additionally, transparency in patent ownership could be improved, making it harder for patent trolls to operate in secrecy.

As for excessive patent monopolies, liberals propose adjustments to patent terms that balance the need for inventors to profit from their work with the broader public interest in access to these inventions. This might include reducing the duration of patents or introducing provisions for compulsory licensing in cases where patents restrict access to important technologies.

A liberal vision for patent reform also recognizes the need for maintaining a healthy competitive environment. This might involve reviewing standards for patentability to ensure that patents are granted only for truly novel and non-obvious inventions, thus preventing the patenting of minor tweaks or existing knowledge which can hamper competition and innovation.

Finally, the government plays a crucial role in this liberal vision for patent reform. Government funding for research and development is seen as vital to fostering innovation. By providing resources for researchers and entrepreneurs, the government can help spur technological progress and economic growth.

In essence, the liberal approach to patent reform is about ensuring that the patent system works as it should: as a catalyst for innovation, not a barrier to it. Through carefully considered reforms, liberals aim to create a patent system that rewards creativity, promotes competition, and serves the public interest.

As we look ahead, the landscape of innovation and patenting continues to evolve at a rapid pace. The advancements in technologies such as artificial intelligence, quantum computing, and genetic engineering are testing the limits of our current patent system. The need for comprehensive and adaptive patent reform becomes even more urgent in this context.

The liberal vision for patent reform will continue to advocate for a balanced and fair system that encourages innovation while ensuring competition. The goal is to create a patent system that not only rewards inventors but also benefits society by fostering access to new technologies and spurring economic growth.

Addressing the issues of patent trolls and excessive patent monopolies will remain at the forefront of this reform effort. Legislative and policy changes will need to be implemented to discourage predatory patent practices and limit monopolies that can stifle innovation.

The future of the patent system will also likely involve a shift towards greater transparency and collaboration. We can expect to see a growing trend towards open patenting and licensing models that foster collective innovation, akin to the Creative Commons approach in copyright.

Finally, as we navigate this uncharted territory, the role of government in supporting research and development will be crucial. Public funding will be essential in driving innovation in areas of significant societal importance such as clean energy, public health, and climate change solutions.

Ultimately, the journey towards patent reform is a journey towards a more innovative, equitable, and prosperous future. The road may be complex and challenging, but the potential benefits for society make it a path worth pursuing.

25: Trademark Reform and Consumer Protection

Trademarks represent more than just symbols, logos, or names; they are a cornerstone of brand identity and play a crucial role in the marketplace by differentiating products and services. From a liberal standpoint, an effective trademark system serves two important functions. First, it protects businesses, allowing them to build brand recognition and consumer trust. Second, it acts as a consumer protection mechanism by preventing deceptive practices and reducing consumer confusion. However, like any system, it's not without its shortcomings.

In this chapter, we will delve into the liberal perspective on trademark reform, with a focus on fostering a balanced system that protects businesses, encourages innovation, and safeguards consumers from unfair practices. We will examine the current challenges that mar the system, from trademark squatting to excessive litigation, and the reforms liberals advocate to create a more fair and accessible trademark system. Furthermore, we will explore how these reforms align with the broader liberal commitment to promoting entrepreneurship, fostering a competitive marketplace, and upholding consumer rights.

25.1: The Role of Trademarks in Business and Consumer Protection

Trademarks lie at the heart of modern commerce, serving as the nexus point between businesses and consumers. They are the visual, textual, or conceptual embodiments of brand identity that differentiate products and services in the marketplace. As such, they are vital to businesses, allowing them to build brand loyalty, reputation, and competitive advantage. But trademarks are not solely about business benefits. From a consumer perspective, they serve as guides, helping consumers make informed purchasing decisions based on brand reputation and quality.

Liberals recognize this dual role and the need for a balanced approach. Protecting trademark rights is crucial to foster a vibrant and innovative business environment. This protection should not just extend to large corporations, but also to small businesses and startups that rely on their trademarks to carve out a niche in competitive markets.

At the same time, the trademark system must prioritize consumer protection. Misleading or deceptive trademark practices, such as counterfeit goods or trademark squatting, can deceive consumers and erode trust in the marketplace. Liberals advocate for strong enforcement measures against these practices to ensure that trademarks remain reliable indicators of origin and quality.

However, the current trademark system faces several challenges, ranging from excessive litigation to issues of accessibility. These issues necessitate reforms to ensure that the trademark system continues to protect businesses, foster innovation, and safeguard consumers. The following sections will delve into these challenges and the liberal vision for reform.

25.2: Current Challenges in the Trademark System

The complexity and fast-paced nature of today's business environment have created unique challenges within the trademark system. For starters, the issue of trademark squatting — registering a trademark without intending to use it, with the sole purpose of selling it or suing potential infringers — has grown substantially. This not only stifles innovation but also results in excessive litigation and financial burdens, particularly detrimental for small businesses and startups.

Another concern within the trademark system is the rise in infringement cases. With the rapid expansion of the digital marketplace, businesses across borders can easily, knowingly or unknowingly, infringe upon established trademarks. This not only results in legal complications but also poses risks for consumers who might be misled by confusingly similar brands.

The liberal viewpoint recognizes these challenges as significant barriers to a fair and competitive marketplace. In response, liberals advocate for comprehensive trademark reforms that aim to curb these exploitative practices. They stress the need for clearer laws around trademark usage and stronger enforcement mechanisms to deter infringers and squatters. Moreover, they underscore the importance of international cooperation in trademark regulation, given the global nature of modern commerce.

Reform isn't just about tackling these challenges, though. It also entails creating a trademark system that is accessible and equitable, allowing businesses of all sizes to protect their brand identities without incurring prohibitive costs. The next section explores these proposed reforms and their potential impacts on businesses and consumers.

25.3: Moving Towards Trademark Reform: Balancing Innovation and Consumer Rights

Liberal thinkers envision a trademark system that provides robust protection for businesses, promotes innovation, minimizes litigious disputes, and places consumer protection at its heart. This vision entails substantial reforms aimed at addressing the systemic challenges within the current trademark system.

First and foremost, they propose stricter laws against trademark squatting. This would deter individuals and entities from registering trademarks purely for financial gain, ensuring that marks are only granted to those with a bona fide intention to use them in commerce. Such a measure could reduce excessive litigation and promote a more innovation-friendly environment.

Second, liberals advocate for a streamlined and more affordable trademark application process. This would level the playing field for businesses of all sizes, ensuring that even startups and small enterprises can protect their brands without being burdened by prohibitive costs.

To enhance consumer protection, they call for tougher penalties for deceptive and unfair trademark practices. This includes misleading or confusing branding that exploits consumers' trust. Also, they endorse clearer labeling requirements to help consumers make informed choices.

Last, they underscore the need for improved domestic and international cooperation in trademark enforcement. Given the global reach of today's digital marketplace, cross-border collaboration is more important than ever in tackling trademark infringement and ensuring a fair and competitive global business environment.

The role of government in this endeavor is paramount. Liberals believe that effective implementation of these reforms requires strong regulatory oversight, along with public and private sector collaboration. By embracing these changes, they argue, we can create a trademark system that fosters innovation, supports businesses, and above all, protects consumers.

As we look ahead, the need for effective trademark reform continues to grow. The complexities of the digital age, the ever-evolving global marketplace, and the rising tide of entrepreneurship all call for a trademark system that is resilient, fair, and consumer-oriented.

The future of trademarks and consumer protection, as viewed through the liberal lens, lies in the balance between protecting business interests and ensuring consumer rights. The aim is to cultivate a marketplace that champions innovation, embraces healthy competition, and shields consumers from deception and unfair practices.

In an increasingly interconnected world, we must recognize that trademark issues are not confined within national borders. The future holds a promise of stronger international cooperation in enforcing trademark rights and protecting consumers worldwide. This will require not only domestic reforms but also collaborative efforts at the global level.

Moreover, we stand at the threshold of opportunities to harness technology to enhance the trademark system. Artificial intelligence, blockchain, and other emerging technologies could be pivotal in improving trademark registration, monitoring infringements, and empowering consumers with information.

Thus, as we move forward, the liberal commitment to trademark reform and consumer protection will remain steadfast. It is an ongoing journey towards a fair, accessible, and effective trademark system that serves the interests of businesses and consumers alike, fostering a thriving and equitable economy in the years to come.

26: Intellectual Property and the Digital Age

The Digital Age, characterized by rapid technological advancements and the proliferation of the internet, has undeniably reshaped society in countless ways. Among these transformations is the profound impact on the realm of intellectual property rights, touching upon copyrights, patents, and trademarks alike. This collision of intellectual property and technology presents a new landscape filled with both challenges and opportunities, where age-old principles meet unprecedented scenarios.

The internet has revolutionized how we create, share, and consume content, blurring the lines of traditional intellectual property paradigms. Concepts of authorship, ownership, and infringement have all come under scrutiny as digital technologies push the boundaries of what is possible. Meanwhile, the global nature of the internet complicates jurisdiction and enforcement of intellectual property rights, demanding international cooperation and harmonization of laws.

In this chapter, we will explore the liberal perspective on these challenges. Recognizing the importance of intellectual property rights in promoting innovation and creativity, protecting creators, and serving public interest, liberals seek to adapt and evolve these rights to suit the contours of the digital landscape. This requires a delicate balance: ensuring adequate protection for creators and innovators, safeguarding consumer interests, encouraging open knowledge and innovation, and promoting fair and equitable access to digital technologies. As we delve into these complex issues, we will consider how intellectual property policies can be modernized for the internet era, and how international cooperation plays a pivotal role in shaping the future of intellectual property rights in our interconnected world.

26.1: Intellectual Property in the Digital Age: Challenges and Opportunities

The convergence of intellectual property rights and the digital world has ushered in a host of new challenges and opportunities. For copyright laws, the internet has facilitated an unprecedented ease of creating, sharing, and accessing content. While this democratization of information offers immense opportunities for creativity and knowledge sharing, it also presents challenges for protecting copyright holders and combating piracy. Similarly, in the realm of patents, digital technologies have spurred extraordinary innovation, yet the pace of technological change often outstrips the legal frameworks designed to protect these innovations.

From a liberal standpoint, the goal is to navigate this digital landscape in a manner that supports innovation, protects creators and consumers, and adapts to the rapidly evolving technological landscape. This involves considering a host of complex questions. How do we balance open access and the protection of intellectual property rights in an era of easy replication and sharing? How should patent laws adapt to accommodate the rapid pace and unique characteristics of digital innovations? How can trademark laws protect brands in the digital marketplace while also preventing unfair competition and deceptive practices?

Moreover, the digital age also presents unprecedented opportunities to leverage intellectual property for social and economic progress. Open source software, Creative Commons licensing, and other alternative models are redefining how we think about intellectual property, fostering collaboration, and democratizing access to knowledge and innovation. For liberals, these shifts are embraced as integral to a progressive and inclusive digital future.

In navigating these challenges and opportunities, liberals advocate for flexible, forward-looking policies that can adapt to the rapid changes in the digital environment. They also emphasize the need for international cooperation, given the global nature of the digital space. The goal is a balanced intellectual property regime that encourages creativity, supports innovation, protects rights holders, and promotes a free and open digital ecosystem.

26.2: Adapting Intellectual Property Policies for the Internet Era

The advent of the digital age has necessitated a rethinking of traditional intellectual property policies. As the internet becomes an ever-more essential platform for the creation and dissemination of knowledge and creative works, it is vital to adapt intellectual property laws to reflect this new digital reality. The ease of duplicating and disseminating digital works, the advent of user-generated content, and the shift towards open source and collaborative modes of creation all pose new challenges and opportunities for intellectual property regulation.

From a liberal perspective, the response to these changes is grounded in a commitment to fostering innovation and creativity, while ensuring that the rights of creators are protected. This involves advocating for copyright laws that strike a balance between protecting original works and allowing for fair use, and patent laws that recognize and incentivize the unique forms of innovation enabled by digital technologies.

Liberals advocate for measures such as the expansion of fair use principles, the adoption of shorter and more flexible copyright terms, and the implementation of more rigorous tests for patentability to prevent the overreach of patent protection in the digital realm. They also support efforts to increase transparency and facilitate access to copyrighted works for educational, research, and non-profit uses, in recognition of the internet's potential as a tool for knowledge sharing and democratization.

In the realm of trademarks, liberals argue for policies that protect brands and consumers in the digital marketplace, without stifering competition and innovation. This includes measures to combat cybersquatting and fraudulent practices, and to adapt trademark protections to the unique features of e-commerce and digital branding.

Overall, the liberal approach to intellectual property in the internet era is one that seeks to adapt to and harness the possibilities of digital technologies, rather than resist them. The aim is to create an intellectual property regime that not only protects creators and innovators, but also leverages the potential of the internet to promote a more democratic, creative, and inclusive digital culture.

26.3: International Cooperation and the Future of Intellectual Property Rights

As the digital age has made borders increasingly irrelevant, intellectual property rights have become a global issue. The internet allows for the instant dissemination of creative works, ideas, and innovations across national boundaries, presenting new challenges for the enforcement of intellectual property rights. In this global landscape, it is imperative that countries cooperate to harmonize their intellectual property laws, combat digital piracy, and ensure fair practices worldwide.

Liberals advocate for robust international cooperation in the field of intellectual property rights. This includes active participation in international agreements and treaties, such as the Berne Convention for the Protection of Literary and Artistic Works, the Paris Convention for the Protection of Industrial Property, and the World Intellectual Property Organization Copyright Treaty. It also involves cooperation to combat digital piracy, which undermines the rights of creators and stifles innovation.

But cooperation is not just about enforcement. Liberals also emphasize the need for equitable practices in the global intellectual property system. This means ensuring that developing countries have access to essential medicines, educational resources, and other patented technologies that are crucial for social and economic development. It also means advocating for fair compensation for creators and innovators around the world, and fostering a global environment that promotes creativity and innovation.

Looking towards the future, the liberal perspective recognizes the potential of emerging technologies to reshape the landscape of intellectual property rights. Innovations such as blockchain technology, artificial intelligence, and advanced data analytics could offer new ways to track, protect, and license intellectual property rights, while also posing new challenges for regulation. In navigating these changes, liberals will continue to advocate for policies that balance the protection of intellectual property rights with the promotion of innovation, accessibility, and fairness.

In the digital age, intellectual property rights are more important than ever. As we continue to navigate the complex intersection of technology, creativity, and law, the liberal commitment to balancing the rights of creators with the public's access to knowledge and culture will remain a guiding principle.

As we stand on the cusp of a future characterized by rapid digital and technological advancements, the liberal perspective on intellectual property rights becomes even more crucial. The digital age has not only revolutionized how we create, share, and consume content, but it has also posed unique challenges to existing frameworks of intellectual property rights. The future will no doubt bring further disruptions and evolutions, and our policies must be ready to adapt and respond.

First, we must continue to strive for the delicate balance between the rights of creators and the public's access to knowledge and culture. The digital age has democratized creativity and innovation like never before, and our policies should foster this environment, not stifle it. At the same time, creators should be justly compensated for their work and assured that their rights are protected.

Second, the future of intellectual property rights must be viewed through a global lens. The internet knows no borders, and neither should our approach to intellectual property rights. International cooperation will be paramount, both in terms of harmonizing regulations and combatting global issues such as digital piracy.

Last, emerging technologies will play a significant role in shaping the future of intellectual property rights. Whether it is blockchain technology that allows for transparent and secure record-keeping, or artificial intelligence that blurs the line of authorship, these innovations will pose new challenges and opportunities for our intellectual property framework.

The liberal approach to intellectual property rights - rooted in principles of fairness, accessibility, and innovation - will be more relevant than ever as we navigate the uncharted territories of the digital future. In this ever-evolving landscape, our aim should be not merely to react to changes, but to anticipate them, shaping an intellectual property system that nurtures creativity and serves the public interest in the digital age and beyond.

27: Understanding Universal Basic Income: A Potential Solution for Economic Inequality

In a rapidly evolving economy marked by growing income inequality, job displacement due to automation, and a fraying social safety net, the concept of Universal Basic Income (UBI) has emerged as a potential solution to these daunting challenges. Proponents view it as a tool that can bridge the income disparity, provide a basic level of economic security, and offer a more equitable future.

From the liberal perspective, UBI aligns with the core values of economic justice and human dignity. Its simplicity, universality, and unconditional nature can potentially transform social welfare and redefine our understanding of work and economic participation. However, it also raises valid concerns and invites crucial questions: Can we afford it? Will it discourage work? What will be the long-term economic and social effects?

This chapter aims to explore these questions and delve into the nuanced debate around UBI within the liberal agenda. It will provide an understanding of what UBI is, explore the potential benefits and challenges it presents, and consider its role in the future of economic policy and security. In this pursuit, we will aim to provide a balanced overview, grounded in the principles of liberalism, while confronting the complexities and uncertainties of this innovative proposal.

27.1: Understanding Universal Basic Income: A Potential Solution for Economic Inequality

Universal Basic Income (UBI) has garnered considerable attention as a potential solution to economic inequality. At its core, UBI proposes a radical shift in our social contract: the idea that every citizen, regardless of their work status, income, or social position, should receive a regular, unconditional sum of money that is enough to cover their basic needs. Advocates argue that this guarantees everyone a basic level of economic security and dignity, a concept firmly rooted in liberal values.

UBI takes various forms depending on the proposals put forth by scholars, economists, and policymakers. Some suggest a complete replacement of existing social safety nets with UBI, while others argue for UBI as an addition to current welfare programs. The funding mechanisms also vary widely, from wealth taxes and carbon taxes to dividends from public resources or sovereign wealth funds.

From the liberal perspective, UBI presents an intriguing solution to the persistent problem of economic inequality. It addresses income disparity directly, by redistributing wealth and providing everyone with a guaranteed minimum income. Furthermore, it offers a safety net that is universal and unconditional, not tied to work or means-testing, potentially eliminating the stigma associated with traditional welfare programs. It could also serve as a buffer against job displacement due to automation and technological advancements, an increasingly relevant concern in the digital age.

However, understanding UBI also necessitates a comprehensive look at the various debates surrounding its implementation. Questions of feasibility, effects on work incentives, and potential inflationary impact are crucial aspects that need thorough exploration. These concerns, along with the examination of UBI trials and their results, will be discussed in the following sections, offering a comprehensive look at this potential tool for economic equality and security.

27.2: The Benefits and Challenges of Universal Basic Income

Universal Basic Income (UBI) offers potential benefits that could drastically reshape our economic landscape. Advocates argue that UBI would not just address poverty and economic inequality directly, but also lead to a range of secondary benefits.

To start, by providing everyone with a guaranteed income, UBI could dramatically reduce poverty and financial instability. It could act as a safety net for individuals during periods of economic upheaval or personal hardship. UBI could also empower individuals to pursue education, entrepreneurial ventures, or other activities without the immediate pressure of earning a living.

Furthermore, UBI could stimulate economic growth. With more disposable income, consumer demand could increase, driving businesses to expand and create jobs. UBI could also serve as an automatic stabilizer in economic downturns, maintaining consumer spending when incomes fall.

However, implementing UBI presents its own set of challenges. The most significant of these is the cost. Financing a UBI that provides everyone with a livable income could require substantial increases in taxation or government debt, both of which could have their own economic repercussions.

There are also concerns about potential impacts on work incentives. Critics fear that a guaranteed income could discourage people from working, although evidence from various UBI trials seems to counter this argument. Most trials have found little to no effect on overall work levels, with some even seeing increases in entrepreneurship as people feel financially secure enough to start their own businesses.

Another point of contention is the potential inflationary effect of UBI. Some economists worry that injecting large amounts of money into the economy could drive up prices, negating some of the benefits of the increased income. However, others argue that this would depend on the specifics of the UBI scheme and the broader economic context, and that appropriate policies could mitigate such risks.

The balance of these benefits and challenges is a subject of ongoing debate among economists, policymakers, and society at large.

Nonetheless, the idea of UBI has sparked a fundamental rethinking of economic security and equality, and its role in our societies moving forward.

27.3: The Future of Universal Basic Income: A Safety Net for All?

As we look towards the future, Universal Basic Income (UBI) continues to be a topic of intense discussion and experimentation. The question remains: could UBI serve as a comprehensive safety net for all, providing economic security in an uncertain future?

In the context of social welfare, UBI represents a radical shift. It promises to simplify the welfare state by replacing a complex web of targeted assistance programs with a single, universal payment. This approach could drastically reduce bureaucratic overheads and deliver assistance more efficiently and equitably.

Economically, UBI could function as a powerful tool for redistribution, helping to combat rising inequality by ensuring that everyone receives a share of the national income. It could also make the economy more resilient, providing a steady stream of income that stabilizes consumer spending, even in times of economic crisis.

In relation to the future of work, UBI is often seen as a response to the potential job displacement caused by automation and artificial intelligence. By providing a guaranteed income, UBI could help to smooth the transition, providing workers with the financial security they need to retrain or adapt to a changing labor market.

Around the world, various UBI trials are underway, testing these theories in practice. These experiments are yielding valuable data on the impacts of UBI, ranging from its effects on poverty and employment, to health outcomes, and even measures of happiness and well-being. Though results are preliminary, they provide important insights for policymakers considering UBI.

Yet, UBI is not without its critics, even within liberal circles. Some argue that it diverts resources away from targeted welfare programs that cater to specific needs, such as housing or healthcare. Others worry about the political feasibility of such a radical reform and the economic implications of funding it.

In the balance of these debates, the future of UBI remains uncertain. However, the conversation surrounding it reflects a broader liberal commitment to confronting economic inequality and ensuring security for all citizens. As we move forward, the ongoing exploration of UBI will undoubtedly continue to shape our vision for a fair and inclusive society.

As we close this chapter on Universal Basic Income and Economic Security, it's important to reflect on the future implications of this novel economic approach.

Our global society is standing at the cusp of a technological revolution, one that will likely have profound impacts on the labor market and the economy as a whole. Automation and artificial intelligence are evolving at an unprecedented pace, reshaping industries and potentially displacing large swaths of the workforce. In this context, Universal Basic Income has emerged as a potential safeguard, a means of ensuring a basic level of economic security in an uncertain future.

Yet, the journey towards implementing UBI, should society choose to undertake it, will not be without its challenges. Economic, social, and political hurdles await, requiring innovative solutions and persistent advocacy. From financing the initiative, to reshaping societal attitudes towards work and income, there is much work to be done.

Furthermore, we must continue to scrutinize UBI through empirical lenses. Ongoing and future UBI trials around the world will provide invaluable insights, shedding light on its real-world impacts and offering guidance for refinement and implementation.

Above all, the exploration of UBI reflects a commitment to reconsidering the foundations of our social contract in a rapidly changing world. It embodies the liberal spirit of innovation and progress, always seeking new ways to build a society that is more equitable, inclusive, and just.

The future of Universal Basic Income is yet unwritten, but its potential makes it a compelling narrative in our ongoing quest for economic security for all. As we look to the horizon, it's clear that UBI will remain a key part of the conversation in the liberal agenda, shaping and being shaped by the future we aspire to create.

28: Military Spending and National Defense

In the vast and complex world of public policy, military spending and national defense often take center stage, occupying significant portions of the national budget. Over time, the traditional approach to these areas has favored increasing spending on the military at the expense of other areas like diplomacy, development, and even domestic needs. However, there is a growing consensus, particularly among liberal thinkers and policymakers, that this trend needs to change.

This chapter aims to illuminate the liberal approach to military spending and national defense, which calls for a rebalancing of priorities that aligns with a comprehensive and sustainable perspective on national security. It argues that our understanding of defense should not be limited to military might alone but should also encompass diplomacy, international development, and strengthening domestic sectors.

We begin by providing a comprehensive overview of the current landscape of military spending, discussing the significant budget allocations and the underlying motivations that drive them. Following this, we delve into the liberal perspective on these matters, highlighting the inherent value in investing more in diplomatic efforts, fostering international development, and bolstering domestic sectors. We detail how this shift in focus can contribute to a more secure and stable world, advancing both national and global interests.

Finally, we discuss the practical considerations of implementing such a policy shift. We explore the potential challenges, from political opposition and economic constraints to security concerns, as well as the strategies that can be used to overcome them. Concurrently, we outline the opportunities that lie ahead, should this more balanced, more holistic approach to national defense be adopted.

Welcome to a nuanced exploration of military spending and national defense, where we challenge the norm, rethink priorities, and imagine a more balanced, secure future.

28.1: Understanding the Current Landscape of Military Spending

Military spending, often seen as the cornerstone of national defense, is an area of public policy that commands substantial financial resources. This allocation, however, is not uniform or static but reflects a complex interplay of economic, political, and security considerations.

Understanding this status quo is crucial for any substantive discussion on reform or change.

In recent years, the defense budget has typically claimed a substantial portion of the national budget, exceeding even the combined total of numerous other domestic programs. These funds are allocated towards a wide variety of areas: personnel and training, research and development, procurement of weapons systems and other equipment, operations and maintenance, nuclear deterrence, and more. The driving force behind these allocations is the perceived need to maintain military readiness, deter potential adversaries, and assert influence on the global stage.

Underlying these allocations are several motivations. The primary one is the pursuit of national security—ensuring the safety and well-being of the nation's citizens and maintaining territorial integrity. This motivation is often extended to include protecting allies and advancing the nation's interests abroad. But beyond security, other motivations come into play. Military spending is also driven by the defense industry's economic influence, the political calculus of elected officials, and the broader geopolitical environment.

The economic dynamics that influence military spending are multifaceted. At one level, defense contracts support jobs and stimulate economic activity, particularly in districts with substantial defense industry presence. These economic considerations often influence politicians' stance on defense spending, with support for robust military budgets seen as a way to protect jobs and stimulate local economies. On another level, spending on defense competes with other national priorities—healthcare, education, infrastructure, and social security, to name a few. Choices in this area reflect the nation's values and priorities, balancing the perceived need for security against other societal needs.

Political dynamics also play a significant role. Military spending decisions are often subject to partisan debates, reflecting differing views on national security, fiscal responsibility, and the country's role in the world. Furthermore, these decisions can be influenced by lobbying from defense contractors, veterans' organizations, and other interest groups.

In summary, the current landscape of military spending is shaped by a complex interplay of factors—economic considerations, political dynamics, and perceived security needs. Understanding this landscape sets the stage for the subsequent discussion on the liberal approach to military spending and national defense, which advocates for a rebalancing of priorities in favor of diplomacy, development, and domestic needs.

28.2: The Liberal Approach: Advocacy for Diplomacy, Development, and Domestic Needs

The liberal perspective on military spending represents a shift from the traditional approach, introducing a broadened perspective on what constitutes national security. It is an outlook that recognizes the need for a strong military but equally emphasizes diplomacy, international development, and investment in domestic sectors. This multidimensional approach positions national security within the wider context of global peace, international cooperation, and national well-being.

One of the core tenets of the liberal stance on military spending is the conviction that diplomacy should be given as much prominence as military might. Diplomacy, from this perspective, is a critical tool for mitigating conflict, building alliances, and fostering international cooperation. By advocating for greater investment in diplomatic efforts, liberals argue for a proactive and preventive approach to national security, one that addresses potential threats through negotiation, cooperation, and mutual understanding.

Similarly, international development is viewed as a key component of a comprehensive security strategy. Investing in the economic growth, health, education, and stability of other nations, especially those in conflict-prone regions, serves to create a more stable global environment. From the liberal viewpoint, such investments reduce the conditions that breed conflict and extremism, such as poverty, inequality, and political instability, making them a viable long-term strategy for national and global security.

Last, liberals argue for increased investment in domestic sectors. They maintain that a nation's security is also determined by the strength of its economy, the health and education of its citizens, the resilience of its infrastructure, and the quality of its social services. Strengthening these sectors not only enhances the well-being of the population but also creates a more robust and resilient nation that is better equipped to face any potential threats.

The liberal approach to military spending, thus, advocates for a more balanced allocation of resources. Rather than disproportionately funding the military, it proposes a distribution that reflects the importance of diplomacy, international development, and domestic investment in ensuring national security. This approach suggests a broader, more holistic understanding of defense—one that acknowledges that a nation's strength lies not only in its military prowess but also in its diplomatic influence, its role in global development, and the robustness of its domestic sectors.

By challenging the traditional emphasis on military spending and presenting a multifaceted approach to national defense, the liberal perspective invites us to reimagine how national security can be achieved, sustained, and made mutually beneficial on a global scale.

28.3: The Road to Implementation: Challenges and Opportunities

Political opposition is a key hurdle to overcome. The liberal approach to military spending can face resistance from those who argue for a continued robust defense budget, viewing it as vital for national security. This opposition can come from various quarters, including politicians with strong defense industry ties or areas heavily reliant on defense jobs. Overcoming this resistance requires sustained advocacy, public education about the potential benefits of a rebalanced approach, and negotiation to secure necessary political support.

Economic constraints also pose significant challenges. Reducing defense spending and reallocating funds to diplomacy, development, and domestic needs might be seen as a risk, especially during periods of economic instability. Moreover, sudden reductions in military spending can impact the defense industry, potentially leading to job losses in the short term. To address these concerns, a phased and strategic approach to budget reallocation might be necessary. This approach could include measures to support affected workers and communities and to stimulate job creation in other sectors.

Security concerns are another significant challenge. Critics might argue that a reduction in military spending could endanger national security by potentially diminishing military readiness or the country's ability to respond to threats. To address these concerns, proponents of a rebalanced approach need to effectively communicate how diplomacy, international development, and domestic investment contribute to long-term security. They also need to reassure that adequate defense spending will be maintained to ensure military readiness.

Despite these challenges, the shift towards a more balanced approach to military spending presents several opportunities. Domestically, funds redirected from the defense budget could significantly improve areas like education, healthcare, and infrastructure, enhancing the overall well-being of citizens and the resilience of the nation. Internationally, increased spending on diplomacy and development could boost the country's global standing, foster stronger international relationships, and contribute to a more stable, peaceful global environment.

Furthermore, potential strategies for overcoming the identified obstacles include fostering broad-based coalitions to support policy change, increasing public awareness of the benefits of a balanced defense approach, and strategically phasing in budgetary shifts to minimize economic disruption.

While the path to implementing a more balanced approach to military spending and national defense is not without obstacles, it is a journey filled with opportunities for positive change. With thoughtful strategies and a commitment to a broader vision of security, it is a road that can lead to a more prosperous, stable, and secure future.

As we conclude this exploration of the liberal approach to military spending and national defense, it is evident that we stand on the cusp of a potential paradigm shift. This shift, from a singular focus on military might to a more balanced and holistic view of defense, is as challenging as it is promising. While the road to this new vision of defense is fraught with political, economic, and security challenges, it is also paved with opportunities for enhanced domestic well-being, more constructive international relations, and a more sustainable, comprehensive approach to national security.

Looking toward the future, it is clear that the traditional understanding of defense, grounded almost exclusively in military spending, is ripe for reevaluation. In an interconnected and rapidly changing world, security is not just about military strength. It is about robust diplomatic relationships that foster mutual understanding and cooperation. It's about investing in global development to create a more equitable and stable world, reducing the conditions that breed conflict and insecurity. It is about recognizing that a nation's strength also lies in the well-being of its citizens, in the quality of its education, healthcare, infrastructure, and social services.

The task for policymakers, thinkers, and citizens alike is to engage in this reimagining process and to navigate the challenges that come with it. A continued dialogue is needed, one that involves diverse voices and perspectives, to ensure that this shift is not just theoretical but translates into practical, beneficial changes in policy and practice.

As we look ahead, the vision of a balanced, comprehensive approach to defense and security is compelling. It is a vision that offers not just a safer and more secure nation but also a more prosperous, equitable, and resilient one. It invites us to embrace a broader, more nuanced understanding of security, one that recognizes our shared vulnerabilities and shared potential. It is a vision that, while challenging to implement, holds promise for a future where defense and security are pursued not just through military might but through diplomacy, development, and the pursuit of domestic well-being. It is a future worth striving for.

29: The Future of the Liberal Agenda

As we cast our gaze forward to the future of the liberal agenda, we find ourselves in a time of profound transformation and possibility. The political landscape is evolving, driven by demographic shifts, changing public attitudes, and emergent challenges that demand innovative responses. Amidst this dynamism, progressive politics in the United States finds itself at an important juncture, tasked with the responsibility of shaping a more just, equitable, and sustainable society.

This concluding chapter of our exploration seeks to map out the contours of this evolving landscape, to identify the trends and challenges that will define the future of the liberal agenda. It is a journey that takes us from the grassroots level, where new voices and concerns are emerging, to the grand stage of national politics, where policy battles are fought and the direction of the country is decided.

Our exploration begins with an examination of the current political environment. We delve into the complexities of the changing liberal base, reflecting an increasingly diverse, informed, and engaged constituency. We identify the issues that resonate with these progressive voters, from longstanding concerns like healthcare, social justice, and climate change, to emerging areas of focus, such as technology regulation, income inequality, and systemic racism.

At the same time, we confront the challenges that stand in the path of the liberal agenda. Political polarization and the influence of money in politics are formidable obstacles, as are the ongoing social and economic disparities that persist in our society. How these challenges are navigated will significantly shape the trajectory of progressive politics in the coming years.

As we stand on the cusp of this future, we invite you to join us in this exploration, to grapple with the complexities, to engage with the challenges, and to envision the possibilities. The future of the liberal agenda is not a foregone conclusion but an unfolding narrative—a narrative that we all have a role in shaping. So, let's begin this journey, as we look ahead, navigate the currents, and chart a course towards a more just, equitable, and sustainable society.

29.1: The Evolving Landscape: Trends and Challenges in Progressive Politics

The liberal base, once seen as a relatively homogenous block, has grown increasingly diverse and dynamic. It is a coalition that crosses racial, ethnic, generational, and socioeconomic lines, reflecting the broad spectrum of American society. This diversity brings a wealth of perspectives, experiences, and ideas to the liberal movement, adding depth and richness to its policy discourse.

A key trend within this evolving landscape is the rising influence of younger generations. Millennials and Generation Z, marked by their progressive attitudes on issues like climate change, racial justice, and economic equality, are becoming politically active and shaping the agenda of progressive politics. They bring with them a renewed sense of urgency and a demand for bold, transformative policies.

Additionally, the growing multiculturalism within the liberal base is becoming a powerful force in progressive politics. Issues of racial justice, immigration reform, and representation have gained prominence, alongside traditional progressive concerns like healthcare, education, and labor rights.

Despite these promising trends, the path ahead is not without challenges. Political polarization is a significant hurdle, as it fosters an environment of opposition and gridlock, making it harder to build consensus and pass legislation. The influence of money in politics is another challenge, with big donors and special interests often having a disproportionate say in political discourse and policy-making.

Economic disparities, both within the liberal base and the broader society, pose further challenges. Despite progress, significant gaps persist in income, wealth, health, education, and opportunities, particularly along racial and ethnic lines. These disparities underscore the urgency of the liberal agenda and the need for policies that promote equity and social justice.

The rise of misinformation and the increasing fracturing of the media landscape is a challenge that impacts the political process. Ensuring accurate information dissemination and fostering productive discourse amidst a deluge of misinformation is an ongoing challenge.

Taken together, these trends and challenges present a complex, dynamic landscape for progressive politics. As the liberal base evolves and expands, it brings to the fore new issues and demands, shaping a progressive agenda that is as diverse and dynamic as its constituents.
At the same time, navigating the challenges of polarization, money in politics, economic disparities, and misinformation will be crucial in translating this agenda into tangible progress towards a more just, equitable, and sustainable society.

29.2: The Core Pillars of the Future Liberal Agenda

The future liberal agenda is likely to be shaped around a constellation of issues that reflect the diverse interests and concerns of its evolving base. While it will continue to champion traditional progressive causes, it will also expand to include emerging areas of focus. Here, we delve into these core pillars that will define the liberal agenda of the future.

Healthcare remains a central issue for liberals, evolving to incorporate broader concerns about public health, mental health, and healthcare equity. The COVID-19 pandemic has further underscored the need for a robust, accessible, and equitable healthcare system. As such, the push for universal healthcare, stronger pandemic preparedness, and health-related social policies is likely to continue to be a cornerstone of the liberal agenda.

Social justice, another longstanding progressive cause, will remain central, but its scope is broadening. Racial justice, in particular, has emerged as a significant area of focus, with a growing demand for policies that address systemic racism, promote police reform, and foster racial equity in education, employment, and housing.

Climate change, already a key part of the liberal agenda, is likely to gain even more prominence. The increasing urgency of the climate crisis has spurred calls for more ambitious and comprehensive climate action, such as the Green New Deal. In addition, the links between environmental justice and social and economic equality are being recognized, leading to a more holistic approach to sustainability.

Income inequality is another area that will remain a focus for the liberal agenda. The widening wealth gap and its impact on economic security, opportunity, and social cohesion will continue to drive calls for progressive taxation, labor rights, and social safety nets.

Emerging areas of focus include technology regulation and the digital divide. As technology plays an increasingly central role in our lives, concerns about data privacy, online misinformation, tech monopolies, and digital access and literacy are rising. These issues bring a new dimension to the liberal agenda, one that intersects with economic, social, and democratic concerns.

Taken together, these themes present a liberal agenda that is rooted in its traditional focus on healthcare, social justice, and environmental sustainability, but is also responsive to the evolving concerns of its base. It is an agenda that seeks to address the multifaceted challenges of our time, from systemic racism and income inequality to the climate crisis and the impact of technology. By doing so, it aims to move us closer to a more just, equitable, and sustainable society.

29.3: Towards a More Just, Equitable, and Sustainable Society: Strategies for Implementation

Successfully advancing the liberal agenda in an evolving and often challenging landscape requires strategic action. In this section, we outline some of the key strategies that can aid in realizing this vision of a more just, equitable, and sustainable society.

Coalition-building is a crucial element in this strategy. The strength of the liberal agenda lies in its diverse base and the broad array of issues it encompasses. Building alliances across these varied interests and groups not only amplifies the collective voice of progressives but also helps foster mutual understanding and solidarity. This could involve creating platforms for dialogue and collaboration among different interest groups, and fostering partnerships between policymakers, activists, academics, and community leaders.

Grassroots activism has always been a driving force in progressive politics, and its role remains vital. By engaging people at the local level, grassroots movements can spur civic participation, influence public opinion, and bring attention to issues that may be overlooked in national discourse. Moreover, these movements can serve as a testing ground for progressive policies, demonstrating their efficacy and building a case for their broader adoption.

Policy innovation is another key strategy. The complex challenges of our time require solutions that are not just effective but also equitable and sustainable. This requires thinking beyond traditional policy paradigms and embracing innovative approaches, whether it's Green New Deal-style proposals for tackling climate change and inequality simultaneously, or new frameworks for regulating technology that balance innovation with privacy and equity concerns.

The role of technology in advancing the liberal agenda also cannot be overstated. From social media activism to digital organizing, technology offers powerful tools for rallying support, raising awareness, and effecting change. At the same time, it's crucial to acknowledge and address the digital divide that can exclude marginalized groups from these digital spaces.

The road towards a more just, equitable, and sustainable society is undoubtedly challenging. Yet, by harnessing the power of coalitions, grassroots activism, policy innovation, and technology, it is a road that can be navigated. The future of the liberal agenda, and indeed of our society, will depend on the commitment, creativity, and solidarity of all those who share this vision. As we continue on this journey, we are not just advancing a political agenda; we are shaping our collective future—a future that values justice, equality, and sustainability, and sees them not as isolated goals, but as interconnected pillars of a thriving society.

As we conclude this journey through the landscape of the liberal agenda, it's fitting that we end by looking to the future. A future marked by the continuous evolution of our societal fabric, our shared values, and the challenges we face as a nation. A future that is ours to shape.

The path forward is layered with complexity and punctuated by the unknown, yet it's also vibrant with potential. The diversity and dynamism of the liberal base promise a future of innovative solutions, robust dialogue, and inspiring leadership. The issues that define the liberal agenda—healthcare, social justice, climate change, income inequality, technology regulation, and more—are not just policy points, but the pillars upon which we build our collective tomorrow.

In this future, the power of grassroots activism is not only preserved but is invigorated, mobilizing individuals to contribute to societal change and inspire a renewed sense of civic responsibility. As the digital realm becomes an increasingly dominant part of our lives, we will need to navigate its implications wisely, leveraging its potential for good while mitigating its risks.

The challenges we face—political polarization, wealth disparities, systemic racism, and the urgent climate crisis, to name a few—are formidable. But they are challenges we must and can address, driven by the progressive principles of justice, equity, and sustainability that form the foundation of the liberal agenda.

We step into this future together, with the shared responsibility to shape it. It's a responsibility that calls upon us to listen and learn, to question and innovate, to build bridges and form coalitions. It's a responsibility that asks us to strive for a future that is not just better for some, but better for all.

As we look ahead, we remember that the future of the liberal agenda—and indeed, the future of our nation—depends on our collective will to envisage and create a more just, equitable, and sustainable society. It's a future worth striving for, a future worth believing in. In the end, our shared vision and our shared efforts shape the path forward. And so, together, we march on.

As we conclude this journey through the liberal agenda, let us remember that change begins with us. It is not enough to simply understand and support the ideas presented in these pages. We must take action, advocate for progress, and fight for the world we envision. Together, we can reshape the narrative, redefine the possibilities, and forge a path towards a future that leaves no one behind.

About the Author

Bradley Hall is a dedicated advocate for change. He follows the dictionary definition of liberal from the Merriam Webster Dictionary, "One who is open-minded or not strict in the observance of orthodox, traditional, or established forms or ways."

With a background as a personal finance expert and a dual expertise as a banker and tax expert, he brings a unique perspective to the intersection of finance and politics. He believes monetary policy and taxes benefit the ultra-wealthy and big businesses to the detriment of the 99%.

During his tenure as the Administrator of the United States Pirate Party from 2009 to 2011, Bradley played a pivotal role in advancing the organization's legislative and political agenda through advocacy initiatives. He drafted articles, letters, reports, and technical documents on policy and public affairs issues, shedding light on the need for copyright reform, patent reform, and enhanced personal privacy protections.

Bradley's passion for political engagement extends beyond his professional roles. He has consistently monitored social media and online sources for industry trends, staying informed about the latest developments in political landscapes. Through his insightful analysis and commentary, Bradley has become a trusted voice in the field, offering critical perspectives on current political issues.

There are those who want to make this country great, "again." But for so many of us, it was never great. But we can make it so.

The American Dream. Plainly, that's what it is. There are no qualifiers, no caveats, no buts.

References and Further Reading

Like most nonfiction books, this book does not stand alone. It is the culmination of many years of reading. Many years of internalizing every book I have ever read. Every argument I have had. Every thought. So it would be difficult to reference sentence by sentence what came from another source and what came from my mind. So I am putting here a list of books that will continue the conversation on the various topics in this book, separated by chapter.

Chapter 2

- El-Sayed, A., & Johnson, M. (2021). Medicare for all. New York, NY: Oxford University Press.
- Colton, D. (2019). The case for universal health care. Clarity Press.
- Reid, T. R. (2010). The healing of America. New York, NY: Penguin.
- Rosenthal, E. (2018). An American sickness. Penguin Books.
- Stiglitz, J. E. (2013). The price of inequality. New York, NY: WW Norton.
- Gore, A. (2006). An inconvenient truth. Emmaus, PA: Rodale Press.
- Klein, N. (2015). This changes everything. Simon & Schuster.
- Yergin, D. (2021). The new map the new map. New York, NY: Penguin.
- Giddens, A. (2011). The politics of climate change (2nd ed.). Oxford, England: Polity Press.
- Weisman, A. (2022). The world without us. Picador.

Chapter 3

- Makary, M. (2021). The price we pay the price we pay. New York, NY: Bloomsbury Publishing.
- Friedman, G. (2020). The case for medicare for all the case for medicare for all. Oxford, England: Polity Press.

Chapter 4

- Wilkinson, R., & Pickett, K. (2011). The spirit level. New York, NY: Bloomsbury Publishing Plc.
- Hickel, J. (2018). The divide. New York, NY: WW Norton.
- Piketty, T. (2017). Capital in the twenty-first century (A. Goldhammer, Trans.).
- Saez, E., & Zucman, G. (2019). The triumph of injustice the triumph of injustice. New York, NY: WW Norton.

Chapter 5

- Hirsch, E. D. (1999). The schools we need. Anchor Books.
- Wagner, T. (2014). The global achievement gap. London, England: Basic Books.
- Wade Boykin, A., & Noguera, P. (2011). Creating the opportunity to learn. ASCD.
- Klein, A. (2008). A class apart. Simon & Schuster.
- Jensen, E. (2019). Handbook for poor students, rich teaching. Bloomington, MN: Solution Tree Press.
- Elliott, W., & Lewis, M. K. (2015). The real college debt crisis. Westport, CT: Praeger.
- Golden, D. (2007). The price of admission. Broadway Books.
- Oneal, A. (2019). Debt-free degree. Ramsey Press.
- DeVitis, J. L. (Ed.). (2022). The future of American higher education. Sterling, VA: Stylus Publishing.
- NC Promise – UNC System. The University of North Carolina System. July 10, 2023. https://www.northcarolina.edu/future-students/nc-promise/

Chapter 6

- Duberman, M. (2019). Stonewall. Plume.
- Alexander, M. (2020). The new Jim crow (10th anniversary edition) the new Jim crow (10th anniversary edition) (10th ed.). New York, NY: New Press.
- Coates, T.-N. (2015). Between the world and me. New York, NY: Random House.
- Oluo, I. (2019). So you want to talk about race. Seattle, WA: Seal Press.
- Eskridge, W. N., & Riano, C. R. (2020). Marriage equality.

Chapter 7

- Smith, J. (2015). Wrongful convictions. North Charleston, SC: Createspace Independent Publishing Platform.
- Banks, B. (2019). What set me free (the story that inspired the major motion picture Brian banks). New York, NY: Simon & Schuster.
- Alexander, M. (2020). The new Jim crow (10th anniversary edition) the new Jim crow (10th anniversary edition) (10th ed.). New York, NY: New Press.
- Mauer, M. (1999). Race to Incarcerate. New York, NY: New Press.
- Armand, I., & Carrington, T. (2018). Levon and Kennedy. New York, NY: powerHouse Books.
- Godsey, M. (2019). Blind injustice. Berkeley, CA: University of California Press.
- Dybdahl, T. L. (2023). When innocence is not enough. New York, NY: New Press.
- Scheck, B., & Neufeld, P. (2000). Actual innocence: Five days to execution and other dispatches from the wrongly convicted. New York, NY: Bantam Doubleday Dell Publishing Group.
- Morton, M. (2015). Getting life. New York, NY: Simon & Schuster.
- Crawford, W. B. (2015). Justice perverted. Amazon Difital Services LLC - Kdp Print.
- Lifton, R. J., & Mitchell, G. (2002). Who owns death? Harper Perennial.
- Trotti, M. A. (2022). The end of public execution the end of public execution. Chapel Hill, NC: University of North Carolina Press.
- Stevenson, B. (2015). Just mercy. Spiegel.
- Gavrielides, T. (Ed.). (2021). Routledge international handbook of restorative justice. London, England: Taylor & Francis.
- Johnstone, G., & Van Ness, D. (Eds.). (2006). Handbook of restorative justice. London, England: Willan Publishing.
- Zehr, H. (2014). Welcome Home diabetic cookbook. Intercourse, PA: Good Books.
- Gould, J. B., & Metzger, P. R. (Eds.). (2022). Transforming criminal justice. New York, NY: New York University Press.
- The Marshall Project. Retrieved July 3, 2023, from https://www.themarshallproject.org/

Chapter 8

- Kennedy, J. F. (2018). A Nation of Immigrants. New York, NY: HarperCollins.
- Golash-Boza, T. M. (2011). Immigration nation. London, England: Paradigm.
- De Forest, G. A. (2016). Strangers in our own lands. Booklocker.com.
- Nayeri, D. (2019). The ungrateful refugee. New York, NY: Catapult.
- Cornejo Villavicencio, K. (2021). The undocumented Americans the undocumented Americans. New York, NY: One World Books.
- Chomsky, A. (2014). Undocumented. Boston, MA: Beacon Press.
- Lee, J. (2012). The diversity paradox. New York, NY: Russell Sage Foundation.
- Shorten, A. (2022). Multiculturalism. Oxford, England: Polity Press.

Chapter 9

- Archer, A., & Kleinman, L. (Eds.). (2022). If I don't make it, I love you. New York, NY: Sky Pony Press.
- Peterson, J., & Densley, J. (2022). The violence project. New York, NY: Abrams Press.
- Klein, J. (2013). The bully society. New York, NY: New York University Press.
- Kopel, D. B. (2013). The truth about gun control. New York, NY: Encounter Books.
- Waldman, M. (2015). The second amendment. Simon & Schuster.
- Cornell, S. T. (2008). A well-regulated militia. New York, NY: Oxford University Press.
- Gold, L. H., & Simon, R. I. (Eds.). (2015). Gun Violence and Mental Illness. Arlington, TX: American Psychiatric Association Publishing.
- Ahonen, L. (2019). Violence and Mental Illness (1st ed.). doi:10.1007/978-3-030-18750-7

- American Psychiatric Association. (1994). Dsm-iv-tr (4th ed.). Arlington, TX: American Psychiatric Press.
- Guttenberg, F. (2023). American Carnage. San Francisco, CA: Yellow Pear Press.
- Melville House. (2020). Too many times (Melville House, Ed.). Brooklyn, NY: Melville House Publishing.

Chapter 10

- Ross, L., & Solinger, R. (2017). Reproductive Justice. Berkeley, CA: University of California Press.
- Boston Women's Health Book Collective, & Norsigian, J. (2011). Our bodies, ourselves. New York, NY: Simon & Schuster.
- Weitz, R., & Kwan, S. (2013). The politics of women's bodies (4th ed.). Cary, NC: Oxford University Press.
- Morgan. (2003). Sisterhood is forever. New York, NY: Simon & Schuster.
- Kay, M. R. (2018). Not light, but fire. York, PA: Stenhouse.
- Romero, M. (2017). Introducing Intersectionality. Oxford, England: Polity Press.
- INCITE! (Ed.). (2016). Color of violence. Durham, NC: Duke University Press.

Chapter 11

- Moore, G. T. (2022). Beyond the voting rights act. Berlin, Germany: De Gruyter.
- Burgan, M. (2015). Voting rights act of 1965: An interactive history adventure. Capstone Press.
- May, G. (2014). Bending toward justice. Durham, NC: Duke University Press.
- Abrams, S., Anderson, C., Kruse, K. M., Richardson, H. C., & Thompson, H. A. (2020). Voter Suppression in U.S. Elections (J. Downs, Ed.). Athens, GA: University of Georgia Press.
- Miller, D. (2019). Voter Disenfranchisement. Cavendish Square Publishing.
- Medvic, S. K. (2021). Gerrymandering. Oxford, England: Polity Press.
- Seabrook, N. (2022). One person, one vote. New York, NY: Pantheon.

- Keena, A., Latner, M., McGann McGann, A. J., & Smith, C. A. (2021). Gerrymandering the states. Cambridge, England: Cambridge University Press.
- Kury, F. L. (2018). Gerrymandering. Lanham, MD: Hamilton Books.
- Levitsky, S. (2019). How Democracies Die. Broadway Books.
- Daley, D. (2017). Ratfucked. New York, NY: Liveright Publishing Corporation.
- Cebul, B., Geismer, L., & Williams, M. B. (Eds.). (2018). Shaped by the state. Chicago, IL: University of Chicago Press.

Chapter 12

- Brimner, L. D. (2022). Strike! Honesdale, PA: Calkins Creek.
- Finkelstein, N. H. (2019). Union made. Highlights Press.
- Guendelsberger, E. (2020). On the clock. New York, NY: Back Bay Books.
- Ehrenreich, B. (2021). Nickel and dimed (20th anniversary edition) (S. Bershtel, Ed.). Picador.
- Bobo, K. (2011). Wage theft America. New York, NY: New Press.
- Galemba, R. B. (2023). Laboring for justice. Palo Alto, CA: Stanford University Press.
- Reyes, T., & Jayaraman, S. (2020). Tipped. New York, NY: New Press.
- West, D. M. (2019). The future of work the future of work. Washington, D.C., DC: Brookings Institution.
- Hogler, R. L. (2015). The end of American labor unions. Westport, CT: Praeger.
- King, M. L. (2012). All Labor Has Dignity. Boston, MA: Beacon Press.

Chapter 13

- Stryker, S. (2017). Transgender history (second edition). Seattle, WA: Seal Press.
- Triska, A. M. (2022). Parenting your transgender teen. Rockridge Press.

- Tannehill, B. (2018). Everything you ever wanted to know about trans (but were afraid to ask). London, England: Jessica Kingsley.
- Gillespie, P. (Ed.). (2023). Authentic selves. Boston, MA: Skinner House Books.
- Marcus, E. (2002). Making gay history. Harper Perennial.
- Faderman, L. (2016). The gay revolution. New York, NY: Simon & Schuster.
- Pitman, G. (2019). The stonewall riots: Coming out in the streets. New York, NY: Abrams Books for Young Readers.
- Duberman, M. (2019). Stonewall. Plume.

Chapter 14

- Alexander, M. (2020). The new Jim crow (10th anniversary edition) the new Jim crow (10th anniversary edition) (10th ed.). New York, NY: New Press.
- Coates, T.-N. (2015). Between the world and me. New York, NY: Random House.
- Oluo, I. (2019). So you want to talk about race. Seattle, WA: Seal Press.
- DiAngelo, R. (2018). White fragility. Boston, MA: Beacon Press.

Chapter 15

- United Nations: Department of Public Information. (2018). Universal declaration of human rights. New York, NY: United Nations.
- Donnelly, J. (2013). Universal human rights in theory and practice (3rd ed.). Ithaca, NY: Cornell University Press.
- Montgomery, J. W. (2019). Human rights and human dignity. 1517 Publishing.
- Kissinger, H. (1994). Diplomacy. New York, NY: Pocket Books.
- Sharpe, S. (2023). Five times faster. doi:10.1017/9781009326506
- Grieco, J., Ikenberry, G. J., & Mastanduno, M. (2022). Introduction to international relations (3rd ed.). London, England: Bloomsbury Academic.

- Mingst, K. A., Karns, M. P., & Lyon, A. J. (2022). The united nations in the 21st century (6th ed.). London, England: Routledge.
- Hanhimäki, J. M. (2015). 7. Reform and challenges: the future of the United Nations. In The United Nations: A Very Short Introduction.

Chapter 16

- Zittrain, J. (2008). The future of the internet--and how to stop it. New Haven, CT: Yale University Press.
- Morozov, E. (2012). The net delusion. New York, NY: PublicAffairs.
- Latkowski, T. (2021). Democracy Vouchers. Democracy Policy Network Books.
- Lessig, L. (2012). Republic, lost. New York, NY: Twelve.
- Lessig, L. (2021). They don't represent us. New York, NY: HarperCollins.
- Levin, Y. (2008). Imagining the future. New York, NY: Encounter Books.
- Holthaus, E. (2020). The future earth. New York, NY: HarperOne.
- Brockman, M. (2011). Future science. New York, NY: Random House.
- Lane, J. I., Fealing, K. H., Marburger, J. H., & Shipp, S. S. (Eds.). (2011). The science of science policy. Palo Alto, CA: Stanford University Press.
- Neal, H. A., Smith, T. L., & McCormick, J. B. (2008). Beyond sputnik. Ann Arbor, MI: University of Michigan Press.

Chapter 17

- O'Brien, A. (2020). The power of green the power of green. Byamyo.
- Riofrancos, T., Aronoff, K., Battistoni, A., & Aldana Cohen, D. (2019). A planet to win A planet to win. London, England: Verso Books.
- Prakash, V., & Girgenti, G. (2020). Winning the Green New Deal. Simon & Schuster.
- Calhoun, C., & Fong, B. (Eds.). (2022). The Green New Deal and the future of work The Green New Deal and the future of work. New York, NY: Columbia University Press.

- Rifkin, J. (2019). The Green New Deal The Green New Deal. New York, NY: St Martin's Press.

Chapter 18

- Gibbs, L., Bainbridge, J., Rosenblatt, M., & Mammo, T. (2021). How ten global cities take on homelessness. Berkeley, CA: University of California Press.
- Winegarden, W., Tartakovsky, J., Jackson, K., & Rufo, C. F. (2021). No way home. New York, NY: Encounter Books.
- Colburn, G., & Aldern, C. P. (2022). Homelessness is a housing problem. Berkeley, CA: University of California Press.
- Eide, S. (2022). Homelessness in America. Lanham, MD: Rowman & Littlefield.

Chapter 19

- Chemerinsky, E. (2021). Presumed guilty. New York, NY: Liveright Publishing Corporation.
- Lessig, L. (2012). Republic, lost. New York, NY: Twelve.
- Levitsky, S., & Ziblatt, D. (2019). How Democracies Die. New York, NY: Crown Publishing Group.
- Cage, J. (2020). The price of democracy the price of democracy (P. Camiller, Trans.). London, England: Harvard University Press.
- MacLean, N. (2018). Democracy in chains. Penguin Books.

Chapter 20

- Assange, J. (2016). Cypherpunks. OR Books.
- Marr, B. (2023). The future internet. Nashville, TN: John Wiley & Sons.
- Susskind, J. (2023). The digital republic. London, England: Bloomsbury Publishing PLC.
- Alegre, S. (2023). Freedom to think. London, England: Atlantic Books.
- Surratt, C. G. (2001). The Internet and Social Change. Jefferson, NC: McFarland.

Chapter 21

- Jamison, K. R. (1997). An unquiet mind. Vintage.
- Harper, F. (2017). Unfuck your brain. Bloomington, IN: Microcosm Publishing.
- Amen, D. G. (2020). End of mental illness, the. Wheaton, IL: Tyndale House.
- Van Der Kolk, B. (2015). The body keeps the score. Penguin Books.

Chapter 22

- Heijnen, E. (Ed.). (2020). Wicked arts assignments. Amsterdam, Netherlands: Valiz.
- Gerber, A. (2017). The work of art. Palo Alto, CA: Stanford University Press.
- Bringley, P. (2023). All the beauty in the world. Simon & Schuster.
- Magsamen, S., & Ross, I. (2023). Your brain on art. New York, NY: Random House International.

Chapter 23

- Rai, A. (2023). Copyright Law in Digital Age. Self Publish.
- Stacey, P., & Pearson, S. H. (2017). Made with Creative Commons.
- McGuinness, P. (Ed.). (2015). Copyfight. Sydney, NSW, Australia: NewSouth Publishing.
- Boyle, J. (2009). The public domain. New Haven, CT: Yale University Press.
- United States Pirate Party. (2012). No Safe Harbor. North Charleston, SC: Createspace Independent Publishing Platform.
- Caso, R., & Giovanella, F. (Eds.). (2016). Balancing copyright law in the digital age. Berlin, Germany: Springer.

Chapter 24

- Understanding patent reform implications. (2009). Eagan, MN: West Publishing.
- Yang, J. (2017). Navigating the patent system. James Yang.
- Duan, C. (2014). A Five Part Plan for Patent Reform. North Charleston, SC: Createspace Independent Publishing Platform.

Chapter 25

- Port, K. L. (2019). Trademark law and policy. Carolina Academic Press.
- Janis, M. D. (2021). Trademark and unfair competition in a nutshell (3rd ed.). Saint Paul, MN: West Academic Press.
- Stim, R. (2022). Patent, copyright & trademark (17th ed.). NOLO.
- Offic, P., & Offic, T. (2010). Us trademark law. North Charleston, SC: Createspace Independent Publishing Platform.
- McLeod, K. (2007). Freedom of expression. Minneapolis, MN: University of Minnesota Press.

Chapter 26

- Guibault, L., & Hugenholtz, P. B. (2006). The future of the public domain. Zuidpoolsingel, Netherlands: Kluwer Law International.
- Halbert, D. J. (1999). Intellectual property in the information age. Westport, CT: Praeger.
- Committee on Intellectual Property Rights in the Emerging Information Infrastructure, Computer Science and Telecommunications Board, National Research Council, & National Academy of Sciences. (2000). The digital dilemma.
- Okediji, R. L. (Ed.). (2018). Copyright law in an age of limitations and exceptions. Cambridge, England: Cambridge University Press.

Chapter 27

- Smith, A. (2019). Universal Basic Income in the United States: Is UBI a Good Idea?
- Choi, J. M., & Murphy, J. W. (1992). The politics and philosophy of political correctness. Westport, CT: Praeger.
- Lowrey, A. (2019). Give people money. New York, NY: Crown Publishing Group.

Chapter 28

- Coyne, C. J. (2022). In search of monsters to destroy. Oakland, CA: Independent Institute.
- Milner, H. V., & Tingley, D. (2016). Sailing the water's edge. Princeton, NJ: Princeton University Press.
- Walzer, M. (2018). A foreign policy for the left. New Haven, CT: Yale University Press.
- Walzer, M. (2023). The struggle for a decent politics the struggle for a decent politics. New Haven, CT: Yale University Press.
- Reno, J. O. (2020). Military waste. Berkeley, CA: University of California Press.
- Thorpe, R. U. (2014). The American warfare state. Chicago, IL: University of Chicago Press.
- Sutten, M., Cousar, C., & Hutchings, R. (2020). Germany. In Modern Diplomacy in Practice (pp. 59–79). doi:10.1007/978-3-030-26933-3_4
- Burns, W. J. (2020). The back channel the back channel. New York, NY: Random House Trade Paperbacks.
- Kissinger, H. (1994). Diplomacy. New York, NY: Pocket Books.
- Miller, T. (2021). Build bridges, not walls. Monroe, OR: City Lights Books.